Thomas Harvey Skinner

The Complaint of the Rev. Thomas H. Skinner

against the Action of the Presbytery of Cincinnati

Thomas Harvey Skinner

The Complaint of the Rev. Thomas H. Skinner
against the Action of the Presbytery of Cincinnati

ISBN/EAN: 9783743378056

Manufactured in Europe, USA, Canada, Australia, Japa

Cover: Foto ©ninafisch / pixelio.de

Manufactured and distributed by brebook publishing software
(www.brebook.com)

Thomas Harvey Skinner

The Complaint of the Rev. Thomas H. Skinner

THE COMPLAINT

OF THE

REV. THOMAS H. SKINNER,

AGAINST THE

Action of Presbytery of Cincinnati,

AT ITS FALL MEETING, 1876,

WITH THE

ARGUMENT.

CINCINNATI:
GAZETTE COMPANY PRINT, FOURTH AND VINE STREETS,
1876.

WITHIN less than a year I have been, three several times, deprived of my constitutional rights as a free Presbyter under the very banner of the Constitution itself. I have earnestly sought amid disorganizing movements to maintain our standards, and the peace, purity, and unity of the Church, in matters of grave moment to every lover of the truth and order of the Presbyterian Church. A just Complaint having been regularly brought by me before the Synod of Cincinnati, and reported as " in order " by the Judicial Committee, and the Synod having voted to hear the Complaint, it was, without even a reconsideration of the vote, turned out of doors, under the pretense of postponement. I, therefore, present to the attention of my brethren the merits of the specific case upon which I asked the Synod to adjudicate. The imputation, gratuitously and injuriously made by the Preamble to the Resolution of the Synod, whereby my Complaint was practically ejected from the House, abundantly justifies me in publishing the Complaint itself and the Argument I had prepared in its support. Neither of them would the Synod even hear. Whether it touches the case of Mr. McCune, every reader may judge for himself. My brethren will decide whether I had just cause of complaint against the Presbytery and whether the Synod could honorably, as a Court of Christ, excuse itself for refusing the hearing I demanded as my right, at its last meeting. They will judge upon whom rests the responsibility of the causes of complaint to the General Assembly.

It has been truly said by one well versed in our ecclesiastical law, " it may be doubted whether a similar arbitrary unconstitutional proceeding can be found in all ecclesiastical jurisprudence of the Presbyterian Church." The law of our Church, publicly cited, repeated, and urged in the Synod itself, declares that " where there is a *right* to appeal and complain, there is *positive obligation* on the part of the judicatory to receive and issue such appeals and complaints;" and that " where ecclesiastical rights of *individuals* or bodies are concerned there is no discretion ; all such rights are guarded by the constitution by which every church court is bound," bound not only to "receive" and "issue," but to "seasonably issue," during the very same meeting of the judicatory, to which the complaint or appeal has been made, the case having been reported "in order," and the records and parties being present. Nothing but "an act of God," unforeseen, or one or other of the grounds of postponement specified in our Digest, none of which existed in this case, is held to justify any departure from this constitutional law. No man may be robbed of his constitutional rights by arbitrary power. Even on the supposition that the McCune case had been pending before the lower court, yet this gave no right for the Synod to eject my Complaint from the house. The Synod had prior jurisdiction. Our Digest tells us that when the pending of one case is set up to defeat another, "the case must be the same: There must be the same parties, or at least such as represent the same interests, there must be the same rights asserted, and the same relief prayed for. The identity in these particulars should be such that, if the pending case had already been disposed of, *it could be pleaded in bar*, as a former adjudication of the same matter, between the same parties." And yet, in violation of these clear principles of righteousness, the arbitrary power of the Synod was used in derogation of my vested ecclesiastical rights, and the Synod ejected my Complaint by an indefinite postponement, upon the excuse of a *perhaps*, which neither civil nor ecclesiastical law would tolerate for a moment. Was not this a living and practical illustration of the doctrine, officially set in circulation by order of the Synod in 1870, that "organic enactments, denominational laws, are the apples of discord and wedges of division in the Christian Church," and ought not to be "enforced?" The end sought was gained, just as the ends sought had been gained in the Presbytery. Nothing is left but to complain to the Assembly. The conduct of the Presbytery for six months, the twice taking from me my right and compelling a complaint to Synod, then the repetition by the Synod of the very offense it was bound to rebuke, and the compulsion again of a Complaint to the Assembly, tells its own story and shows where the responsibility rests. I might plead that the Synod's action was either a prejudice in favor of Mr. McCune, or against myself, or both. I leave this for others to determine.

A generation ago, the Presbyterian Church was torn by the very principles and course of action which have agitated our ministry and Churches within the bounds of the Synod of Cincinnati, giving rise to excesses and disorganizing movements for years past, in connection, among other things, with temperance crusades, women's preaching, unlicensed evangelism, and anti-denominational organic union. These excesses and movements, and the practical destruction of a part of our Presbyterian government, with tendencies antagonistic to the whole of it, I felt myself called upon, with others, in conscience and loyalty to our Church, publicly to oppose.

Therefore, to relieve myself of what I deem an unjust imputation, implied in the resolution passed by the Synod, and to vindicate my own honor, in the character of my Complaint against the Presbytery, to that body, all the more that the Presbytery is now about to enter upon Mr. McCune's case, I publish my own Complaint and Argument for the consideration of all concerned, as also for the information of the Church. I append my protest against the Synod's action, and my Complaint against the Synod to the General Assembly.

T. H. S.

COMPLAINT TO THE SYNOD.

The undersigned respectfully complains to the Synod of Cincinnati against the following action of the Presbytery of Cincinnati, during its sessions at its stated fall meeting, at Mt. Auburn, September 13 to 15, inclusive, and at Cincinnati, October 3 to 5, inclusive, to wit:

I. *In sustaining the decision of the Moderator, whereby my Preamble and Resolutions upon the case of Mr. McCune were ruled as out of order, because they were assumed to be unconstitutional.* The "point of order" (so called) was raised by Dr. Morris, as follows: "That the Preamble and Resolutions just presented by Dr. Skinner can not be considered by this body, on the ground that such consideration would be in violation of the constitutional rights of the Rev. W. C. McCune, and would be a virtual trial of the said Mr. McCune, without due regard to the forms provided for in our constitution." "The Moderator returned to the Chair and announced his decision of the point of order, as follows: 'The point of order is *well taken*, and the Preamble and Resolutions are not in order.' The decision was appealed from, and the Moderator sustained."

My reasons of complaint against this action are:

1. It was a *repudiation by Presbytery* of its *vested constitutional right* (Form of Government, Chapter X, Section 8) "to condemn erroneous opinions which injure the purity or peace of the Church," apart from judicial process against the author.

2. It was a *violation of parliamentary rule*, in derogation of my constitutional right to introduce said Preamble and Resolutions, and to discuss the merits of the same after they were seconded, and I was entitled to the floor, no matter what their fate might have been on the final vote, after discussion.

3. Said decision of the Moderator, sanctioned and sustained by Presbytery, was an exercise of the most responsible prerogative re-

served to the General Assembly, viz.: that of deciding upon questions of constitutional law, and binding its interpretation on the court as a rule of action.

4. It was turning a constitutional question into a parliamentary rule of order, so inventing a new rule, in derogation of my constitutional and parliamentary rights.

II. *In accepting, and thereby making official documents of, the Special Report and Collaterals of the Committee of Investigation in the case of Mr. McCune, without any action whatever to amend or to rectify statements, judgments, and personalities, therein contained, at variance with righteousness and truth.* The Report accepted, Record, p. 217.

My reasons of complaint against this action are:

1. The Report opens with, and its recommendations rest upon, statements contrary to truth.
2. It steps out of its way to raise a new case, instead of confining itself to the terms of the resolution under which the committee was appointed.
3. It implies a censure upon the undersigned, and recommends the Presbytery to pass a judgment which also implies a censure.
4. Part of the Collaterals indulge in gross personalities against the undersigned, which would not be tolerated a moment in debate, and ought not to be tolerated in an official document.

III. *For adopting an answer to the protest of the undersigned, September 15, 1876, Mt. Auburn, without rectifying its erroneous statements and the false impression it is calculated to make.*

My reasons for complaint against this action are:

1. Said answer does not accurately represent the facts of the case.
2. It represents the undersigned as being out of order and furnishing reasonable ground for the annoyances and unlawful interruptions under which he was forced to retire from the floor of the Presbytery.
3. No withdrawal of the protest, for alteration, on account of misrepresentations in the answer, could make the protest "more agreeable" to the "views" of the undersigned.

This Complaint is respectfully submitted, with the request that it may be prosecuted immediately, according to the discipline of our Church.

THOMAS H. SKINNER.

CINCINNATI, October 14, 1876.

THE ARGUMENT.

Mr. Moderator, this Complaint limits itself, specifically, to two things: (1.) To the denial of my constitutional and parliamentary rights as a Presbyter, guaranteed to me by the standards of our Church and our accepted rules of parliamentary order. (2.) To the impeachment of my conduct and character as a man and as a minister while in the public defense of these rights, as also in the public defense of our Presbyterian faith and order. It impinges, in no respect, upon the *merits* of the case of the Rev. Mr. McCune, now in judicial process before the Presbytery of Cincinnati. It relates solely to myself and the Presbytery. This Complaint, Mr. Moderator, needs no apology. The utmost effort has been made, by various parties, to try and degrade the great cause of Truth and Order, out of which this Complaint has sprung, to the aspect of a mere personal quarrel. "The Address to all the Churches of North America," by the advocates of anti-denominational organizations; the wide-spread advocacy of the principles involved herein by so-called Christian Church Union journals, to which the names and influence of many Presbyterian ministers are given; the existence and character of a new organization of this kind in the very bosom of the Presbytery of Cincinnati, with its published Declaration and Basis; the multiplied utterances of the press throughout the land, both secular and religious, and the action of the Presbytery itself instituting inquiry into the merits of this movement, are an abundant answer to so gratuitous a conception. I need, therefore, say no more on this point. There are three separate counts in the Complaint I bring before you: (1.) As to my constitutional and parliamentary rights. (2.) As to the acceptance of the Committee's Report and its Collaterals. (3.) As to the adoption of the answer to a protest. I complain, *first*, that my rights have been wrested from me; *second*, that my conduct and character are impeached in accepted and official documents of the Presbytery, contrary to all precedent. Such is my Complaint.

I. The first point of the Complaint is against Presbytery's action "in sustaining the decision of the Moderator, whereby my Preamble and Resolutions upon the case of Mr. McCune were ruled as *out of order*, because they were assumed to be *unconstitutional.*" (1.) The first reason in support of this first point is that such action, assuming such unconstitutionality, was "a *repudiation*" *by Presbytery of its vested constitutional right* (Form of Government, Chapter X, Section 8) " to condemn erroneous opinions which injure the purity and peace of the Church, apart from judicial process against their author."

I wish it to be distinctly understood by the Synod, that the ground on which the Presbytery's action rested was not the mere *inexpediency* of the application of non-forensic or episcopal power to the condemnation of Mr. McCune's errors and irregularities, but it was the denial that such episcopal power, so to do, did exist by the constitution. If the constitutional power to condemn widely-spread errors, apart from judicial process, had been recognized, no ground would have existed on which to raise a "point of order," or decide any one "out of order" who sought to persuade Presbytery to *exercise* that power, and save a tedious, unnecessary and vexatious litigation. The only question that could have arisen, was, is it "wise, equitable, and for the edification of the Church," to exercise this power, and to this point my Preamble, Resolution, and Argument were directed; *i. e.*, to a discussion of the merits of the case, in view of the Committee's official report, furnishing the "facts" in the case by order of the Presbytery, after five months' investigation. If deemed contrary to the constitution, irregular, unwise, inequitable, and not for edification, after hearing my argument, to *exercise* this power, it was competent to vote down my motion, or lay it on the table; but I assert it was an outrage upon all my rights to shut my mouth, a second time, upon a debatable motion, duly seconded and read, absolutely in order, and on which I had already proceeded to speak. At the Glendale Presbytery, April 13, 1875, the plea of official ignorance was made. The information I came forward to offer was declined. It was said I could not speak on the merits of my Preamble until the *"facts"* were brought in by a Committee. The Committee of Investigation, consuming the summer, reported the *"facts,"* September 13, 1875, indorsing Mr. McCune's course at Linwood and Mt. Lookout, and although themselves disapproving *some* of his views, yet reccommending no disapproval by the Presbytery, but suggesting process against myself for slander. The report was not adopted, but accepted. It was a discussion of the merits of the case by Mr. McCune and the Committee. I then took the official documents, and sought by a Preamble and Resolution, to have Presbytery disapprove both the views and course of Mr. McCune, and forbid their continuance. My mouth was a second time stopped, on the merits of the case, although having the floor, under a debateable motion and perfectly in order. What was accorded to a Committee and to Mr. McCune apart from judicial process, was denied to me. To support what policy, and in whose interest all this was done, I leave others to judge. The refusal to "consider" my Preamble and Resolutions was an oppression. To accomplish this, it was necessary to find some ground on which to raise a "point of order." I announce to the Synod that the very constitution itself was declared unconstitutional, and on that ground I was pronounced out of order, and my rights to discuss the merits of the case, after Mr. McCune had discussed them several hours before Presbytery, and the Committee's report had discussed them, was wrested from me. It is of this injustice I complain, all the more that the Committee itself had intimated to the Presbytery not to have "a judicial trial," and had not even recommended a disapproval of Mr. McCune's "views," and had actually indorsed his "course" at Linwood and Mt. Lookout. It alters not the injustice of the proceeding, that, after much effort to throw this grave matter out of court, and suggest action against myself for the public defense of my rights and the honor of my Church, it was finally considered expedient to institute process against Mr. McCune. The ground on which I was ruled "out of order" was not the inexpediency of exercising the non-judicial power of the Presbytery in condemnation of the errors before us, but the *denial* of that power altogether, and on that ground wresting from me my right of discussion. The reactionary half-recognition of the episcopal power of the Presbytery came later, only in order to furnish a basis for the opinion of its non-applicability to the case in hand, and a justification of judicial process, but not to allow me any right of discussion on the merits of my Preamble and Resolutions. My Complaint, I think, is understood. I shall show that the Presbytery has the very power it repudiated, that I was in order, .and that the action of the Presbytery was an oppression, twice repeated.

Has the Presbytery the constitutional power to condemn erroneous opinions and irregularities of practice, which disturb the tranquility of the Church, apart from tedious and extreme forensic process? My conviction is clear that it not only has this right, but it is in duty bound to exercise it for the edification of the body of Christ; and I think I shall be able to justify this conviction, deep-seated and ineradicable as it is, by the best of evidence and sound argument. I shall adduce in support of my first reason the organic law of the Church itself, established precedents, approved, selected, and recorded since the reunion, in our Digest, for our guide, and by the recognized practice of all courts in their interpretation of constitutional law.

The whole power of jurisdiction and order, vested by Christ in the Church of God on earth, and iu every branch and denomination of it wherever found, is of divine right and origin, and is limited alone by the sovereign authority of the Lord Jesus Christ. It is for the edification ●f His spiritual body and not for destruction. Supervisory and authoritative, it is broad as the inspection and control of the whole Church and adequate to all her wants and necessities. Its exercise is directed to two things, the preservation of the heavenly doctrine in its purity, and the guardianship of the Christian conduct; in other words, to faith and morals. Take these two things away, truth and duty, and neither Form of Government nor Code of Discipline has any value. The written Constitution of the Presbyterian Church, with its system of doctrine and polity, we declare to be "agreeable to the Word of God," and vow to maintain and enforce it as the law of the Church, just because we so believe. Ministerial and declarative alone, and unfettered by human commandments, and neither legislating nor binding by virtue of human authority, nor against the revealed will of God, it is the vice-regal function of the Church, derived from the crown of Him on whose shoulders is the government, who holds the key of David, and who has said, "I give to you the keys of the kingdom. Whatsoever ye shall bind on earth shall be bound in heaven, and whatsoever ye shall loose on earth shall be loosed in heaven." It is an awful and solemn trust, and not a "popish usurpation," to be executed in view of our accountability to Christ for the manner in which we defend the heavenly doctrine and the order of the heavenly house.

The most general, or the generic, name of this power is *"Episco-pal."* It is the exercise of that *watch* and *control* which are given to those whom Christ has appointed and the Holy Ghost has chosen to be ordained "overseers" (*Episcopoi.* Acts xx. 28; 1 Tim. iii. 1, 2) and "shepherds" in the Church. It is sometimes called *"Paternal"* power, in allusion to 1 Tim. iii. 4, 5. Modified as to the method of its exercise, in certain extreme cases, by judicial forms and rules of procedure, it is called *"Judicial"* or *"Forensic."* It is the broadest, most comprehensive, and far-reaching function of government and administration that exists; the most indispensable to the very existence of the Church itself. It is the character of all her action. Deny to the Church of Christ episcopal power, and she is stripped at once of the very means of her self-preservation; her oversight and control are alike wrecked, and not even a shadow is left on which to shape her judicial. But this is so plain I need not argue it. Enough to say that it is by virtue of this episcopal power alone, apart from judicial forms, the power of supervision or inspection, declarative and authoritative, and put by Christ in ordination and the laying on of hands upon the shoulders of every presbyter-bishop, whether teaching or ruling, and vested in every ministerial court, the Church of Christ executes nearly the whole of her divine commission. By this she preaches the gospel, administers sacraments, admits members and ministers into the Church and dismisses them, examines, licenses, puts, or refuses to put, calls into the hands of her ministers, elects, installs, ordains, translates, and removes both ministers, elders, and deacons. By this she forms and dissolves pastoral relations, organizes, visits, unites or divides, and commands Churches, redresses evils, and does whatever pertains to their welfare. By this she requires candidates to pursue certain studies and report their progress to her courts, and calls upon her ministers to give account of their work in the vineyard of the Lord. By this she erects and convenes her courts, frames rules, and subjects to review and control their records and proceedings. She warns against transgression, by this same power, admonishes, reproves, rebukes, exhorts, entreats, enjoins, defends the faith, directs the conduct, decides cases of conscience, suppresses schismatical controversies, arrests lawless practices against her polity, resolves questions of doctrine and discipline reasonably proposed, condemns erroneous opinions, and bears public testimony against whatever she regards as injurious to the faith and order of God's house, and to good manners, charity, truth, and holiness. And all this simply by preamble and resolution, motion and overture, act, testimony, and deliverance, memorial, recommendation, and injunction ;—not by process and verdict. Valid documentary evidence and present undeniable facts, in her own court, have the sanctity and force of a true witness. Moderator, who is it that denies the episcopal power of the Church of Christ? or the episcopal power of every court in it? As well deny that the sun shines in the heavens! Why sir, what kind of power was it the Committee of the Presbytery exercised, in approving the "course" of Mr. McCune, and disapproving his "views" apart from judicial process, and under a Preamble and Resolution of Investigation? What kind of power is it that the editor of the *Herald and Presbyter* exercised? And is any one so forgetful of all consistency as to aver that the Presbytery itself has less power than a mere Committee, the creature of its own appointment, or than the individual editor of a religious newspaper, both using, in full, the name of the author, and affirming a judgment upon the merits of the case? How preposterous to think that in the grave matters that so often engage her

attention in a wicked world, where the adversary ever works to corrupt
her faith and destroy her order, the Presbyterian Church is tied, by
every considerable transgression, to an extreme forensic process, that
may consume a year for its issue, and in the end the remedy prove
worse than the disease! What a harvest of practice for the contentious
and obstinate, unwilling to be reclaimed by milder means! What a
premium on discord! What a plight for the Church of Christ in the
hands of him who, abhorring "*judicial*" power and crying for " peace
and safety" in the midst of fast coming calamities, denies the " *Episcopal*" power too! Then, what is left but fire and stubble? Moderator,
the compass of 1834 will not do for either you or me to steer by in present or coming storms! It is a question if the anchor of Reunion will
hold us, for the gale is strong!

But the Church is not so bound. The recognition of this episcopal
power is inscribed in the constitution, in express terms. "It belong-
eth," says our admirable Confession, Chapter XXXI, Section 2, " to
Synods and Councils, ministerially to determine controversies of faith
and cases of conscience, to set down rules and directions for the worship of God, and government of His Church, which decrees and determinations, if consistent with the Word of God, are to be received with
reverence and submission, not only for the agreement with the Word,
but also for the power whereby they are made, as being an ordinance
of God, appointed thereunto in his Word." The same episcopal power
is expressed again in our Form of Government, Chapter X, Section 8,
which recognizes the "power" vested by Christ in the Presbytery, not
merely to " issue appeals, from church sessions and references brought
before them," nor merely to "judge ministers" by forensic process, but
also, and by a discriminating clause, "to resolve questions of doctrine or
discipline, seriously and reasonably proposed, to condemn erroneous
opinions which injure the purity or peace of the Church, * * and
to order whatever pertains to the spiritual welfare of the churches under her care." Again, with unmistakable emphasis does our Book
of Discipline, Chapter I, Section 5, revolt against the idea that the
Church is tied to extreme forensic process in the exercise of her power,
when it declares that, "the exercise of discipline in such a manner as
to edify the Church, *requires not only much of the spirit of piety, but also
much prudence and discretion.* It becomes the rulers of the Church,
therefore, to take into view all the circumstances which may give a
different character to conduct, and render it more or less offensive;
*and which may, of course, require a very different mode of proceeding in
similar cases, at different times,* for the attainment of the same end."
What could be more explicit? Again, the same power, apart from

judicial process, is recognized as belonging to our General Assembly. Form of Government, Chapter XII, Section 5: "To the General Assembly also belongs the power of deciding in all controversies respecting doctrine and discipline; *of reproving, warning, or bearing testimony against error in doctrine, or immorality in practice, in any Church, Presbytery or Synod;* of suppressing schismatical contentions and disputations," etc., etc. Thus is this episcopal power *common* to all our courts, without exception, for the Presbytery is only a larger session, and the Synod a larger Presbytery, while the Assembly is the crown of all. Will any one say that before error in doctrine and practice, in any member of a Presbytery, can be condemned, or the Presbytery arrest lawless movements and condemn erroneous views of its members, or bear testimony against error rife in the Presbyterian Church, forensic process against their *author* must be commenced and concluded? It is *not* the doctrine of the Presbyterian Church. The best interpretation of any organic instrument or statute is the practice of its framers in the generation contemporaneous with and succeeding its adoption, and the best evidence of that practice is the action of the administering courts themselves, and the decrees and determinations of the supreme court of the Church, which have all the force of constitutional law. " *Contemporanea expositio est optima et fortissima in lege*"—contemporaneous exposition is the best and strongest interpretation in law; this is a maxim of acknowledged validity, universal and conclusive. The construction of the constitution by the courts contemporaneous with its enactment is the surest construction, and next to this, the practice of the courts succeeding. Such judicial interpretation obtains the force of constitutional law itself.

I appeal, therefore, to five celebrated cases in our Digest which testify to the practice of the Church from its very beginning in this land, following the practice of its parent source and which remains alike for all future time, notwithstanding the momentary obscurations of 1822 and 1834, which only prepared the way for an intenser brightness. And all the more I do this, again, at this time, inasmuch as it has been wildly asserted in the lower court, that the exceptional decisions of 1822 and 1834 are to-day accepted law by "ninety-nine hundredths of the Reunited Church." I need only advert to them briefly; they are the cases of Harker, Davis, Balch, Craighead and Barnes. All these began with the direct exercise of episcopal power, apart from judicial process; some of them began, continued, and were concluded by that power alone; while others, which beginning with that power and failing by this milder means to secure the peace and purity of the Church, were concluded by forensic adjudication.

1. *Harker.*—Moore's Digest, p. 218; Baird's Digest, p. 604. In conformity with the early practice of the Church, a non-judicial reference was made to the Synod by Presbytery respecting Mr. Harker, who had "imbibed and vented certain erroneous doctrines." "In 1761, Mr. Harker printed and published his views, and Synod appointed a committee *to examine the book*, who reported next year. The Synod proceeded to consider Mr. Harker's principles, *collected from his book by the committee*, which are in substance as follows." After examination, the Synod passed the following judgment, without any judicial process whatever. "The Synod judge that these principles are of a hurtful and dangerous tendency, giving a false view of the covenant of grace, etc., etc., and that they are contrary to the Word of God and our approved standards of doctrine." On the further consideration of the case, the Synod made the following judgment, to wit: "That Mr. Harker has for several years past been dealt with in the tenderest manner, etc., etc., but that instead of succeeding in these attempts, he appeared to be rather confirmed and resolute in propagating his opinions among the people, etc., etc. On the whole, though the exclusion of a member be grievous, yet we judge that the said Mr. Samuel Harker can not be consistently a member of this body, and accordingly declare him disqualified for preaching and exercising his ministry," etc. Such was the case. The fathers of the Church exercised their episcopal power in "condemning erroneous opinions," and finally excluded a contumacious member, apart from judicial process.

2. *Balch.*—Moore's Digest, p. 220; Baird, p. 614. Mr. Balch, in 1797, having imbibed Hopkinsian doctrines, propagated them, causing a schism in the Church, and the erection of a new independent organization. The "creed" of Mr. Balch, gathered by a commission, was referred to the General Assembly, without any judicial process against its author, asking that the author be required to "acknowledge before the Assembly that he was wrong in the publication of his creed, renounce the errors pointed out, engage to teach nothing hereafter of a similiar nature, and that the Moderator admonish him," etc. Mr. Balch acknowledged his errors: "I do fully acknowledge," etc., did "cheerfully renounce them," did "solemnly and sincerely engage," etc., did "cheerfully submit himself to admonition," and was declared "in good standing in the Church." It was an exercise of episcopal power by the fathers of the Church, under the organic law of the Church.

3. *Davis.*—Moore's Digest, p. 222; Baird, p. 634. The Second Presbytery of South Carolina, in the exercise of its episcopal power, "represented" to the Synod that Mr. Davis, belonging to the First Presbytery, was permitted to "pass without censure, though known to

teach erroneous doctrines on some fundamental points." Synod required the Presbytery to "attend to this matter." After various efforts, charges were tabled by the Second Presbytery, and abandoned, Mr. Davis being excused from censure, on the ground of "liberty of opinion." Synod then commenced a "judicial investigation," and, finally, referred the matter to the Assembly. The Synod's action was declared irregular in proceeding to such judicial investigation, when there was "no reference and no appeal," and the next Assembly refused to "reconsider." This action was just, because the Synod was not a court of original jurisdiction over a minister. It, however, considered an "*overture*" from the Synod of the Carolinas, "requesting their attention to a late publication of the Rev. W. C. Davis, denominated the *Gospel Plan.*" The finding upon the overture was, that the doctrines of Mr. Davis are "contrary to the Confession of Faith and the Word of God," "of very dangerous tendency," and the "Assembly do judge, and do hereby declare, that the preaching or publishing them ought to subject the person or persons so doing, to be dealt with by their respective Presbyteries according to the discipline of the Church relative to the propagation of errors." Judicial process was commenced in a new Presbytery, to which Mr. Davis was attached, his former Presbytery having been dissolved. Mr. Davis declined jurisdiction and was deposed from the ministry. The fact is patent that by episcopal power the errors and course of Mr. Davis were condemned, upon overture alone, apart from the conduct of a regular judicial trial.

4. *Craighead.*—Moore's Digest, p. 223; Baird, p. 638. Mr. Craighead having preached a Pelagianizing sermon before Synod, in 1806, "the things he uttered before the Synod were immediately submitted to that court by the *Committee of Bills and Overtures.*" (Princeton Review, October, 1847, p. 196.) He was admonished on the spot, formally by the Synod, in the exercise of its episcopal power, through the Moderator, to abstain from the propagation of his views. He "set at naught the admonition" of the Synod, determined to keep on in his way, and published the sermon. Judicial process was afterward resorted to. In the course of it, the Assembly said, in 1824, "The Synod might have proceeded instantly to condemn the errors of Mr. Craighead's book, as the Assembly did the "*Gospel Plan*" of W. C. Davis," that is, even without judicial process. (Baird, 642.) It recognized the right to exercise episcopal power, not only in the condemnation of error, but for a "lofty and independent spirit, that would not be controlled by authority," from "a bold and confident controvertist, who sets his opponents at defiance."

5. *Barnes.*—Moore's Digest, p. 226; Baird, p. 650. In 1829, Mr.

Barnes preached the " Way of Salvation," the sermon causing public discussion. Next year the Presbytery of Philadelphia allowed a call from the First Church of Philadelphia to be placed in his hands. A minority protested and complained that the proper consideration of his views was suppressed, and the right of the Presbytery to pronounce upon those views, apart from judicial process, denied. Synod sustained the complaint of the minority, and enjoined Presbytery " to hear and decide on their objections to the orthodoxy of the sermon of Mr. Barnes, and to take such order on the whole subject as is required by a regard to the purity of the Church and its acknowledged doctrines and order." Obedient to this injunction, Presbytery, apart from judicial process, " entered into an examination of Mr. Barnes' sermon, and decided as follows : Presbytery, etc., " are of the opinion that it contains speculations of dangerous tendency," etc. (reciting the points), and, " on the whole, express their deep regret that Mr. Barnes should have preached and published a discourse so highly objectionable," etc., " and earnestly recommend to Mr. Barnes to reconsider and renounce the erroneous matter," etc., and appointed a committee to wait upon Mr. Barnes, and report the result of their interview at the next meeting. Mr. Barnes refused to hear the committee, resisted the exercise of the episcopal power of the Presbytery, pronouncing " the whole proceeding unconstitutional " This was falling back, not on the early practice of the Church, but upon a new interpretation of the constitution given in 1822. The whole matter was now referred directly to the General Assembly of the Presbyterian Church, with the following question, viz.: " Whether, by the constitution, it is competent to any Presbytery to take up and examine any printed publication, and to pronounce it to be erroneous or dangerous, if they so find it, *without in the first place commencing a formal prosecution of the author*, even supposing it to be known and admitted that the author is a member of its own body; or whether a Presbytery, in every such case, *must*, when disposed to act on the same, *forthwith commence a forensic prosecution of the author* of the publication which is believed to contain erroneous and dangerous opinions or doctrines ? " Baird, pp. 654, 655. It is the question of episcopal power, as to its extent, raised in 1831, notwithstanding the previous and uniform practice of the Church, save once, in 1822, which was counteracted by the action of 1824.

The following correspondence with one well qualified to judge in the matter presented, I here insert:

18

CINCINNATI, October 15, 1876.

BRO. BAIRD: Will you be so kind as to give me your opinion in respect to the five cases—Balch, Davis, Harker, Craighead and Barnes—named in the Digest, and state whether they are cases in which the *episcopal power* of the Presbytery, in so far as it may be distinguished from judicial or forensic process, was exercised.

Yours fraternally, etc.,

*   *   *

CINCINNATI, October 16, 1876.

DEAR BROTHER: By "judicial or forensic process" I understand you to mean, proceedings implying the presence of a prosecutor and defendant and forms, the essential features of which are stated in our book, in the chapter on Actual Process.

Episcopal jurisdiction, as contrasted with this, must mean that authority by which, without an intervening prosecutor, or the forms of actual process, Church courts act immediately and of their own knowledge for the correction of disorders, the reclaiming of wanderers, and the protection of the Church and its doctrines.

Of proceedings of this kind, respecting which you inquire, the records of the Church exhibit a number of memorable examples. Conspicuous among them are the cases of Harker, Balch, Davis, Craighead and Barnes. In each of these cases the episcopal authority was employed in examining and censuring the published opinions of the parties. In the Harker case, the Synod, without any of the forms of actual process, having first censured Harker's book, eventually excluded him from the ministry for contumacy and persistency in error. In the other cases, the episcopal function was exercised in censure of the publications, and its action was followed, more or less directly, by measures of forensic or judicial process.

Two other signal examples of episcopal jurisdiction you will find in the New Light and Cumberland Schisms. In both instances the Synod of Kentucky asserted direct episcopal authority over unsound ministers, citing them to its bar, examining them as to their opinions and conduct, and suspending them from their ministry. And in both cases the General Assembly, after mature inquiry into the whole proceedings, fully approved them.

I could mention other instances, but these may serve you as examples of the whole. In fact, it is, I think, beyond question that in all periods of the history of our Church, from the beginning until a comparatively recent date, the episcopal function was in constant exercise, and its righteousness unquestioned by any.

Yours, very truly,

SAMUEL J. BAIRD.

The fortunes of this new movement, that sought to confirm a novel and unwarranted interpretation of our organic law, I need not recount.

19

They are spread at length in Baird's Digest, pp. 650 to 733, to which Moore's Digest, p. 226, refers, traversing a painful conflict of seven years. It was a time of trouble. Must the author of every erroneous and dangerous sentiment be put on trial before the errors of his publications, whether by book, or pamphlet, or newspaper, and his irregularities, be condemned? To what, in troublous times, would the Church be reduced, save a police court or an arena of interminable strife?

The answer of the Assembly of 1834 to the above question, an answer which led directly to the disruption of the Church, because it denied to the Church her right to condemn erroneous opinions apart from the arraignment of the author, was in these words : "That in the opinion of this Assembly, to take up, and *try*, and condemn, any *printed publications* as heretical and dangerous, is equivalent to condemning the author as heretical ; that to condemn heresy in the abstract can not be understood as the purpose of such trial; that the results of such trial are to bear upon, and seriously to affect, the standing of the author; and the fair and unquestionable mode of procedure is, if the author be alive and known to be of our communion, to institute process against *him*, and give *him* a fair and constitutional trial." Baird, p. 669 (8). The peculiar introduction of the word "*try*," in its technical meaning, and in an illegitimate application to the phrase, "*printed publications*," as though any court could ever dream of instituting forensic process against a *book*, an *opinion*, or a *thing*, is evidently inappropriate. The protest to this answer was this : " We protest, because in our judgment this decision not only establishes a principle erroneous in itself, but does in fact the very thing which it imputes to the memorialists; it casts censure on a former General Assembly for examining and condemning a heretical book before the author was tried and condemned by his Presbytery. We here refer to the case of W. C. Davis." Baird, 671.

I gladly and thankfully pass over the history. Would there were nothing here to recall the past! In 1834 the exercise of the episcopal power, in this respect, was *denied*. In 1835, and in 1837, it was triumphantly *reaffirmed* by the Presbyteries in General Assembly. I quote the action of the Assembly of 1835: "*Resolved* that, in the judgment of this General Assembly, it is the right, and may be the duty, of *any* judicatory of our Church to take up, and, if it see cause, to bear testimony against any printed publication which may be circulating in its bounds, and which in the judgment of that judicatory may be adapted to inculcate injurious opinions, and this whether the author be living or dead, whether he be in the communion of this Church or not, *whether he be a member of the judicatory c ing the opinion, or of some other.* * * * To deny to our judicatories, as guardians of the churches, this right, *would be to deny to them one of the most precious and powerful means of bearing testimony against dangerous sentiments,* and guarding the children of the Church against "that instruction which causeth to err." No counter decision to this has ever been made. The action of the Assembly of 1836, of which my own father was the author, and which I well understand, did not antagonize with the definitive action of 1835, which is a precedent that can not be set aside in the Reunited Church. Just what the Assembly of 1836 did, was simply to maintain that, to episcopally condemn the errors of a publication, which errors the Assembly had already decided not to be errors, *after* the formal judicial trial of their author for the same, was improper, and in contravention of the rights of the author, as also a reversal of its own decision upon the merits of the errors themselves. Baird's Digest, p. 694 (3, 4, 5). Whatever difference of opinion might have existed as to the errors themselves, there can be no doubt that the position taken was correct, and in this view I have the sanction of my father himself.

What then, Moderator, is the result we have reached? It is no less than this: (1.) That the express letter of our constitution asserts the right of every one of our Presbyteries and of other courts to condemn error in doctrine and irregularity in practice arising therefrom, apart from judicial arraignment of the author. (2.) That our earlier and later assemblies and inferior courts have done this very thing, not merely "*in the abstract,*" as in the cases of Universalism and Socinianism, etc., but in the concrete, in any publication, whether book, sermon, or pamphlet, set on foot by any one, dead or alive, member of a Presbytery or not, and referring to the publication by title and to the author of the publication by name. (3.) That five memorable historic precedents or actual cases in court confirm and illustrate this exercise of episcopal power; and (4.) That judicial process against the author, or, in other words, the judicial arrest of the person, whether by responsible prosecutor or by common fame, instead of the examination and disapproval of the thing, is not the first but always the last resort; and this I affirm is the genius of our constitution, an instrument framed and fraught alike with the spirit of wisdom and charity, conservative alike of its doctrine and order and the standing of our ministry, the best possible means to save both the Church and her public teachers from defection and destruction.

And now, Moderator, this is the law of our Church, its established law, by the perpetual power of the standards, by memorable expositions and precedents in all our courts, contemporaneous with and succeeding the enactment of our constitution, and by the latest as well as earliest deliverances of our supreme court. I advance *now* to say, that it is the law of our Church, established triumphantly also by the maxims of common law and common sense, as well as by the universally recognized rules and decisions of all civil courts, where contradictory decisions have existed in the same court upon questions of law over which the court has proper jurisdiction. It has been confidently asserted in the Presbytery that the decision of 1834 is the law of the Presbyterian Church, and so regarded by "ninety-nine hundredths" of the reunited body—a marvelous assertion, truly! Certainly the novel interpretation of 1822 was slain by the latter contrary interpretation of 1824. Upon what principle, may I ask, is that of 1834 exalted in force above the still later and contrary interpretation of 1835 in the undivided Church? Not, certainly, upon any principle of legal interpretation, either literal, rational, historical, or mixed. Not, certainly, upon the ground of the early practice of the Church, uninterrupted until 1822. Such logic is in face of all reason, all law, all sense, and is repugnant to the rule accepted by all judges and enforced in all civil courts. "*Stare decisis et quieta non movere*"—to stand by the decisions and not to disturb rights and principles at rest—is an acknowledged rule. Judicial interpretations of the constitution, contemporaneous with its enactment and giving the sense of its framers, will be upheld. The construction of the law by the courts having jurisdiction in the case, at the time and afterward, is the surest and best construction, and no modal limitation is to be inferred which may defeat the plain intent of the law. A principle once established and continued, under the construction of the supreme court which has jurisdiction over questions of constitutional law, is to be maintained as the law of the land. The construction of the court obtains the force and acquires the sanction of constitutional law itself. While the constitution remains unchanged the construction remains unchanged also. "*Stare decisis*"—abide by the decisions. Otherwise a change of construction, in the interest of any excitement, strikes at the foundation of all principles and all rights confirmed under the previous construction and opens the door to interminable strife. The Assemblies of 1822 and 1834 violated this wholesome maxim. They did not "abide by the decisions." They did disturb the "principles and rights at rest." They uttered contradictory decisions to the old, and paved the way for what followed. Contemporaneous exposition was against them. An uninterrupted practice until 1822 was against them. It was incumbent on the Assemblies of 1835 and 1837, in the yet undivided Church, to reclaim and reinstate the early and true construction of the clause in our constitution, which acknowledges the vested right of Presbytery "to condemn erroneous opinions which injure the peace and purity of the Church," and set aside the interpretation of 1834, or else allow the new construction, antagonistic to the plain intent of the law and the whole spirit of our constitution. For who does not know that, where contradictory decisions exist, the " *last decision*" is always in force until reversed. Again I invoke the acknowledged maxims of law by which the courts of law are governed : "*Judicia posteriora sunt in lege fortiora*"—the later decisions are the stronger in law ; "*Judiciis posterioribus fides est adhibenda*"—full faith is to be had in the later decisions; "*Judicia posteriora priora abrogant*"— later decisions annul the earlier contrary ones. Nothing is more settled. The last decision of the Supreme Court of the United States on a question of constitutional law will stand and be respected as against any former contradictory one, and the same is true of the last decision of the General Assembly, the supreme court of the Church, in its construction of the clause in question. Just as in legislation a later statute repeals the former contradictory one, so in adjudication the later judgment of the court annuls the prior ones in conflict therewith ; and this is true in cases both of original and appellate jurisdiction. The last decision of the General Assembly is final, authoritative, and binding on all inferior courts over which it has jurisdiction, whether Synods, Presbyteries, or Sessions.

By what right, then, Moderator, in law, in logic, in reason, in sense, or history, can any one assert that the decision of 1834 is of supereminent authority and binding force, as against the later decision of 1835, which occurred in the undivided Church? Does opposition to the decision of 1835 constitute law, especially when no counter subsequent decision of the Assembly is to be found? All the more, again, by what right, when, by the very terms of our Reunion, we accept as law that which was legally established antecedent to the division of 1838, and our "Concurrent Declarations" affirm that the rules and precedents of each branch of the Church, only subsequent to that division, shall not be regarded as law, unless "approved by both the bodies" and "re-established in the united body?"

The use, by Presbytery, of an author's *name*, or of his publication, in condemning erroneous doctrines, publicly propagated by book, pamphlet, newspaper, and circulated over the author's own signature, or preached from the pulpit, advocated in special lectures on the platform, and advertised from place to place, can form no valid matter of objection to the exercise of episcopal power. It is only what occurs in every public discussion and literary criticism of the works of theologians and moralists. The author uses it himself, and is well known. The position that to condemn the erroneous *opinions* or *doctrines* of a man is to condemn the *man himself as a heretic*, is uncharitable, unhistoric, unscriptural and illogical;—uncharitable to the court, for it subjects the court to the imputation of an attempt to secure, by indirection, a censure of the author, which it may fail to gain by judicial action, so forcing a construction of the act of the court that can not be justified;—uncharitable, also, to the author, for it labors to carry over to the author, who is always more and better than his errors, a disapproving judgment that bears against the errors alone. It is unhistoric and unscriptural, for, in all ages of the Church, apostolic and post-apostolic, and under all forms of discipline, only he is called a " heretic " who obstinately and contumaciously declines to hear the admonition of the Church. So Bingham shows, as I shall hereafter quote. So the Apostle instructs us: "A man that is a heretic, after the first and second admonition, reject." It is illogical on many accounts, for it assumes that a judgment against erroneous doctrine is a judgment against the person, character, and standing, of the author. And yet, in the same breath, severe judicial process is invoked to secure the very end apparently so much deplored! This is inconsistent, for surely the exercise of authoritative non-judicial power is milder and more tender than the exercise of forensic procedure,—for while a judgment against the author, by judicial process, aims at the person, character, standing and usefulness of the *man*, a judgment against the *thing* alone, leaves the person, character, standing, usefulness untouched. Pride may object, but neither justice nor reason can. Peter's standing was not impaired by Paul's reproof at Antioch, neither were the churches of Cilicia and Syria injured by the injunction of the Jerusalem Council.

The objection, moreover, assumes that because the author of error is under the jurisdiction of some Presbytery, therefore no judgment can emerge against his error, except upon judicial process. Formal verdict of "guilty," as in the case of "crime," must be found and formally declared. The whole man and his opinions must be so chained together, under the categories of moral guilt and crime, that no admonition may be allowed, and no injunction be imposed, except upon a personal conviction. That is, the mere fact of jurisdiction, or jurisdiction, *ipso facto*, compels extreme forensic process. But this is a *petitio*. Jurisdiction does not, *ex necessitate*, compel forensic process against the author. It is simply a *dictio juris*, or saying of the law, that both the man and his doctrines are amenable to the authority of some particular court, to be dealt with in any one of the different constitutional modes deemed best for the edification of the Church. Jurisdiction imposes no necessity for this, rather than that, procedure. Such necessity rests on other grounds.

The objection still further assumes that the clause, Form of Government, Chap. X, Sec. 8, means only a condemnation of error *in thesi*,—in other words, the Presbytery is shut up either to judicial arraignment of the author, or to a deliverance against an abstraction. But what is the character of this abstraction ? Where shall we find it ? Where there is jurisdiction in cases of erroneous doctrine, it binds to judicial process, it is alleged. The logical consequence of this is, there can be no such thing as a condemnation of error in the abstract *inside of the Presbyterian Church*, no matter how wide-spread or rife it may be, for all persons inside the Presbyterian Church are under its *jurisdiction*, and where there is jurisdiction over error, judicial process, it is argued, must obtain. Fate is not more inevitable than the logical conclusion from these premises, that *" error in the abstract"* means error *outside* of the Presbyterian Church, that is, *outside of its jurisdiction.* The Presbyterian Church, therefore, can condemn erroneous opinions, rife in her own bosom, in no other way than by the judicial trial, *in detail*, of every man who holds them, *because* every man is under her jurisdiction ! Condemnation of error *in thesi*, therefore, means condemnation of error *outside of the Presbyterian Church !* And this is what is meant by the clause in Form of Government, Chapter X, Section 8 ! The whole authoritative character of the Presbytery, in relation to error in doctrine, inside of the Church, is reduced to judicial process. To such absurdity are we brought by objecting to the use of a *name !* See Baird's Digest, p. 669 (8); 672, §120 ; 730, §168; 731 (4). Against such illogical position the decision of 1835 was directed ; a decision still of binding force. It is gratuitous to say that the clause, Form of Government, Chapter X, Section 8, means *only* condemnation *in thesi*, whether inside or outside our jurisdiction. The book does not say so. The interpretation is a gloss, not an exposition ; a modal limitation upon the law, imported into the text, not drawn from it ; a restriction of its broad intent, which no jurist would decree as just. Action *in thesi* is included, but the vested power of the Presbytery, under that clause, is not limited thereto. The criticism, that the exercise of episcopal power against error would cast some *reflection* on the author, is sentimental. It is the duty of Diotrephes, Alexander the coppersmith, Demas, Hymeneus and Philetus, to make such reflection impossible. But what is the reflection in this case compared with it in cases judicial ?

The objection, moreover, is theologically untenable. Nothing is clearer in the doctrine of Christ, than that the *errors* and *sins* of a believer are constantly condemned before God and the world, while to the person and standing of the believer there is "no condemnation" whatever. This one fact alone is conclusive proof of the incorrectness of the position that the condemnation of error is equivalent to the condemnation of its author. Were such a position true, in itself, or relatively, it would not be possible for God to condemn sin, in the believer, without condemning the *person* of the believer at the same time. It is bad theology. It is as bad polity. The spirit of the polity of Christ is in harmony with the spirit of the doctrine of Christ, and not against it. It is the grace of the gospel-doctrine that intervenes to protect the *person* of the believer, while it condemns his sins. It is the same grace of gospel-polity that intervenes to protect the not yet contumacious person of the teacher, while yet it condemns his errors. It is lawful, right, wise and expedient, to condemn the error and irregularity of any member of Presbytery, without arraigning his person in formal trial before a judicial bar.

Thus, the whole objection is uncharitable, unhistorical, unscriptural, and rests upon prejudices, assumptions, sentimentalisms, importations, illogical inferences, and irrelavent conclusions—all confronted by the letter of the constitution, the nature of the power vested in the Church, by apostolic example, by the precedents of our court, and by the doctrine of the Gospel itself.

The fundamental false postulate upon which the whole objection rests, and to which every argument of the objecter returns, is the denial, outright, of the *authoritative* character of episcopal or paternal power, confining that authority to judicial determinations, and restricting the idea of "discipline" to forensic process. It divests the testifying function of the Church of its whole *authoritative* value, reducing her witness for the truth of Christ, to mere advice, to be rejected or received, at will. It denies the binding nature of that testimony. It makes it simply moral suasion, man's word, not God's demand. In dealing with error everything not judicial is called *advisory*. It is a compromise with Independency—pure Brownism. It denies that the Church is the steward of God invested by Christ, ministerially, to rule the understanding, conscience, and belief of man, and dictate, according to God's Word, what shall be maintained as truth and what condemned as error, apart from judicial process. It asserts that, save in a case of judicial process, the *authority* of the Church in reference to error amounts to a mere power of *advice*, in other words, no authority whatever—a power binding none, but a mere opinion, to be entertained or not, at pleasure. It lifts the voice of remonstrance against the authoritative exercise of the very power Christ has delegated to His Church, as an invasion of the rights of ministers and men, a power so abundantly illustrated by the Church, in all ages. It exclaims against *authority* where forensic forms are wanting. It relegates public offenses against the truth to the category of private ones, then challenges the right of court, or minister, to prosecute, unless some private injury has been received. It deems a private conference and explanation, with liberty abundant still to teach the error, an all-sufficient satisfaction to the Church and to the truth. It holds that admonition and injunction can never be employed for the arrest of error, till all judicial forms have been exhausted. Its tendency is evil. It disintegrates, demoralizes. It mars the sense of solemn obligation, creates indifference to vows, hostility to creeds, invites debates on things forever settled; degrades the ministry, destroys its influence, corrupts the Church, depreciates the truth of God, disputes the law of Christ, and grieves the Spirit of all grace. It ends, at last, in open insubordination, and resistance to all authority, judicial and episcopal alike. History repeats itself, and wisdom may take lesson from the past.

But, Moderator, in addition to all I have said, I would emphasize the fact, already alluded to, that the whole episcopal power the Presbytery possesses to condemn error in doctrine and practice, apart from forensic forms, so far from being unconstitutional, is grounded in that solemn evangelical commission which Christ, the Head of the Church, gave to His apostles, and, through them, to the gospel ministry for all time. In four passages of the New Testament (Matthew xvi. 19 ; Matthew xviii. 18; Matthew xxviii. 19, 20; John xx. 21–23), the charter for the whole disciplinary power of the Church is contained. It relates, not to extraordinary and miraculous endowment, peculiar to apostolic times, but to ordinary and perpetual functions, durable to the world's end. This plenary power, thus delegated by Christ to the apostles, each minister possesses to its whole extent. Will any one be so foolish as to say that, under such a charter, a Presbytery, Synod, or General Assembly possesses less power, less authority, than is given by Christ to each one of the individual members composing it, or that such power is only to be exercised under judicial forms, for the preservation of truth and the suppression of error? Was it forensic process, think you, of which the Saviour spoke when He lifted up His hands on Olivet to bless His chosen, while His feet parted from the mountain and a cloud received Him out of their sight? Sir, it was a gift of episcopal power from the "chief Shepherd and Bishop" of our souls, bequeathed to ordained overseers of the flock, and adequate to all the necessities of the Church henceforth and for evermore—an authoritative power of instruction, inspection, and government, to be executed in His name. And well did the first princes in the Church understand their commission. Were Simon Magus, or the incestuous Corinthian, served with an ecclesiastical libel, and allowed a year and a half, or two years, of judicial process, through ascending appelate courts, before a conclusive sentence overtook them? Were the erroneous opinions of Judaising and Gnosticising teachers, who ventilated their soul-subverting words and walked disorderly, tabulated into formal accusations, witnesses cited, cross-examinations had, wranglings perpetuated, two appeals taken, and bitter parties formed, before the errors themselves were condemned? Did Paul sist Peter in a judicial process at Autioch for his half Christian conduct and time-serving dissimulation? Was Titus commanded to institute judicial investigation against public offenders before he dared to "admonish" them, or "rebuke them sharply" and "before all," that they might be "sound in the faith?" Think you the apostle reluctated to mention the names of Hymeneus and Philetus, Alexander and Demas, Hermogenes and Phygellus, or note by special designation the "unruly and vain talkers and deceivers of the circumcision, whose mouths must be stopped, who subvert whole houses, teaching things which they ought not, for filthy lucre's sake?" Was there any "*reflection*" here? Or think you that the Lord Jesus himself, in glory, deemed it "unconstitutional" and "out of order" to spot "that woman Jezebel" in the church at Thyatria, or name the Balaamites in Pergamos, before a responsible prosecutor had stood up, or formal charges had been preferred? No, Moderator, it was an exercise of episcopal power, as I have said, by the chief Shepherd and Bishop of our souls, who walked unseen among the golden candlesticks and said, " I know thy works."

The Thessalonian Church was enjoined to " warn them that are unruly." Must judicial process be commenced by the Presbytery of Thessalonica? The Corinthian Church is enjoined "not to company with" the gross offenders named by the apostle. Must the offenses be first proved by judicial process against the offenders? The Ephesian Church is enjoined " to have no fellowship with the unfruitful works of darkness, but rather reprove them." Was it that Presbytery must meet and institute a judicial process before admonition or injunction could go forth? Timothy and Titus are ordered to "rebuke openly, before all, them that sin, that others may fear." Has a Presbytery less power than Timothy or Titus? "A man that is a heretic, after the first and second admonition, reject." Did the Presbytery refuse to admonish or reject until after judicial process? The Roman Church was enjoined "to mark them which cause divisions and offenses, contrary to the doctrine" they had learned, and "avoid them." Was it to be done only after judicial process? John enjoins the whole Church not to "receive into the house," nor salute, a corrupter of the truth. Was it an injunction to institute judicial process? The truth is that the administration of godly discipline for the preservation of the truth and morals of the Church is by episcopal function, apart from forensic forms, except in the last resort. It is of the same nature as that of a father over his own house, who, having learned to rule well therein, "knows how to take care of the Church of God."

Who were the "some among you" in the Corinthian Church who denied the resurrection? Were they not as distinctly marked by these discriminating words as were the Cretan "slow-bellies and liars" themselves? What kind of power was it the Jerusalem Council exercised under a non-judicial reference from Antioch, against "certain men" well known, who accounted circumcision more than Christ and His cross, and preached without restraint their soul-subverting doctrine? Was it error only "in the abstract" that council condemned—error, evasive of all allusion to its propagators, or its reported relation to the particular Church at Antioch? Was forensic process ordered to be instituted against the Judaizers or those who had imbibed their false teaching? No. Episcopal power was invoked, the power of the Jerusalem Presbytery, as such, and exercised to its œcumenical extent. Error in doctrine and practice was condemned. The emissaries of Judaism, from their headquarters at Jerusalem, "false brethren, unawares brought in, who came in privily to spy out the liberty" of Gentile Christians in "Christ Jesus, that they might bring them into bondage," were put under the ban. The Churches in Antioch, Syria, and Cilicia were all admonished and enjoined, apart from forensic procedure. Verse 24th of the fifteenth of Acts is a simple *preamble;* verse 29th is simply a resolution of *injunction.*

If we do but read the Scriptures carefully, we shall find that the discipline of the Apostolic Church confined itself to *admonition* first of all, solemnly and twice repeated, before procedure to greater severities. We shall next detect the more impressive *warning* that followed; then the sharp *rebuke* and the authoritative *injunction* against both error in doctrine and practice, by the sole exercise of episcopal power, vested by Christ in His chosen ministry, apart from all judicial process. We shall then learn that it was *contumacy* against such admonition, warning, rebuke, and injunction, that paved the way for *excommunication.* If judicial process ever entered it was only after all other means had been exhausted. Surely, if in the case of *notorious* error, like that of

Simon Magus, or *notorious* practice, like that of the "incestuous" man of Corinth, the notoriety of the fact, or what was "commonly reported" *and known to all as true*, made the offender, *ipso facto*, liable to excommunication, what folly it is to deny the Church's right of mere admonition and injunction when common fame and documentary evidence in court, bright as daylight, make the case beyond dispute!

The history of the sub-Apostolic Church, long before the existence of Theodosian and Justinian codes with civil penalties for error, only confirms the interpretation I have given of the exercise of episcopal power. Errors in doctrine and practice were condemned, uniformly, before extreme process was instituted against their authors. "The directions," says Bingham (Antiquities, II, p. 891), "were drawn up upon the models of those rules of the Apostles which forbade Christians to give any countenance to notorious offenders." "Errorists are they who, when they are reproved for their unsound opinions, *contumaciously resist*" (II, 981). The offenders were named, their errors condemned, and the Churches were warned and enjoined as well as the offender himself, who was admonished or rebuked. It is the doctrine of the Presbyterian Church, framed upon the Apostolic model, in all times and countries, and signal examples of which are found in all her history. "It thus appears," says Sir Henry Wellwood Moncrief, convener of the General Assembly of the Free Church of Scotland, "that the Free Church, by retaining the old form of process as part of her law, *would restrain a Presbytery from instituting or entertaining a regular process against any minister until all means have been exhausted for preventing the necessity of such a process being entered on.*" (Practice of the Free Church, Edinburg, 1871, p. 118.) It is the assertion of episcopal power as lodged in the Presbytery, and precisely to the same end is the comment of Stewart of Pardovan, the Blackstone of the Presbyterian Church, in his "Methodised Observations" upon the clause in our Form of Government, Chapter X, Section 8, giving power to the Presbytery to "condemn erroneous opinions which injure the purity or peace of the Church"—upon which he says that the Presbytery has not only the power of "*censuring ministers,*" of "rebuking gross or contumacious sinners," but also the power "of answering of questions, cases of conscience, solving of difficulties in doctrine or discipline, with petitions from their own or those in other Presbyteries, *examining and censuring according to the Word of God any erroneous doctrine which hath been publicly or more privately vented within their bounds,* and the endeavoring, the reducing, and conversion of any that remain in error and schism." (Obser. Method., Book I, Title XII, Section 4.)

How different from our practice, that would do nothing except resort to judicial process in the very start! Deprive the Church of Christ of her right to bear testimony against and condemn error in doctrine and practice, vented in her own bosom, apart from judicial process, to admonish, warn, reprove, rebuke, enjoin ; deny to Presbytery this right, a right accorded to every pastor and elder by the Word of God, and enforced in every Apostolic letter, and the mission of the Church, as a witness for the Truth, its pillar, ground, and guardian, is concluded forever. With this, therefore, I close the discussion of the first reason to the first point of my Complaint, by affirming that the action of the Presbytery of Cincinnati was a repudiation of the right vested in it by the Head of the Church, to condemn erroneous opinions which injure its peace and purity, a right guaranteed by the constitution itself and protected by parliamentary rule.

(2.) The second reason in support of my first point of Complaint is, that the action of Presbytery, sustaining the decision of the Moderator (see first point of Complaint), was *"a violation of parliamentary rule, in derogation of my constitutional right* to introduce my Preamble and Resolutions, and to discuss the merits of the same after they were seconded, and I was entitled to the floor, no matter what the result might have been on the final vote, after discussion."

I claim, Moderator, that, when I was interrupted on the floor of the Presbytery by Dr. Morris, who rose to a " point of order," asserting that my Preamble and Resolutions were *unconstitutional*, and, therefore, that even the " consideration" of them was not to be entertained, and when the Moderator of the Presbytery decided that the point was *" well taken,"* and the Presbytery *sustained,* on appeal, this decision, I was perfectly "in order." The rules in order in both houses of Congress, in our State Legislatures, and in deliberative bodies in general, are derived from the British Parliament, and modified to suit our various circumstances. The rules of order for our Church judicatories have the same origin. We have thus acquired a system of parliamentary regulations, prescribing and defining a certain fixed mode of procedure in the course of deliberative business. Our general rules of order, which form no part of the Constitution of the Presbyterian Church, as the Constitution of the Presbyterian Church forms no part of them, are inscribed in our Digest, pp. 204 to 208, and are forty-three in number. As to the order prescribed in "judicial process," I do not hear speak. It belongs to the process itself, Presbytery acting as a court, and not as a deliberative and parliamentary body. According to Rule of Order XIV, whenever a motion is made, seconded, written, and read aloud, and the mover addresses the Moderator (Rule XXXI), being entitled to the floor, he conforms to the rules of order laid down for the guidance of our courts. My Preamble and Resolution were in writing; they were duly seconded; no other business was before the house, and I was entitled to the floor by the Moderator's decision, none disputing it; I addressed the chair; 1 was respectful to my brethren. The Investigating Committee had reported, and the official documents necessary to sustain my Preamble and Resolutions were upon the table, subject to the call of myself or any member of the body. I had not only a constitutional right to introduce a Preamble and Resolutions, the object of which was to disapprove erroneous opinions already disapproved of by the Committee itself, but also a parliamentary right to debate the Preamble and Resolutions themselves *upon their merits.* There are two classes of motions, both of which are in order, but only one of which is in order to be discussed upon their merits; in other words, there are motions *debateable* and *undebateable.* In conformity with all parliamentary manuals, our rules of order specify both. (See Rule XVIII.) The motions *undebatable* on their merits are: " to lay on the table," " to take up business," " to adjourn," and " the call for the previous question." All other motions, without exception, are *debateable on their merits.* No power can deprive a man of his right to debate a debateable motion. My Preamble and Resolutions, therefore, were not only " in order," according to our rules, but debateable on their merits by the same rules ; and this is a universal rule. (See the Manuals of Jefferson, Cushing, Roberts, and Warrington, on "Motions.") I was " in order." I had violated no parliamentary rule of procedure in business. The action of the Presbytery, sustaining the Moderator and declaring me " out of order," was, therefore, itself, a *violation* of parliamentary rule in derogation of my constitutional rights of free discussion on the merits of the case before us. It was abundantly competent for the Presbytery, after I had been heard, to make their assumed unconstitutionality of my motion their reason, if they saw fit, for voting down my motion, and putting my Preamble and Resolutions out of the house. But, 1 submit that such assumed unconstitutionality was no reason whatsoever why, when perfectly " in order," I should have been pronounced " out of order," as at a previous Presbytery, and thus twice be denied both my constitutional and parliamentary rights to debate the merits of my motion. I shall return to this again. 1 was perfectly " *in order.*"

(3.) The third reason in support of my first point of Complaint (see first point of Complaint) was, that " said decision of the Moderator, sustained and sanctioned by the Presbytery, was an exercise of the most responsible prerogative reserved to the General Assembly, viz.:

that of deciding questions of constitutional law and binding its interpretation on the court as a rule of action." Individual Presbyteries or Synods have no right to bind their interpretations of constitutional law as a rule of action on the court, much less, where the supreme court itself has, after a sharp contest, announced a definitive decision, and applicable precisely to such cases as the one referred to in my Preamble and Resolutions. It matters not, that a person, charged with teaching erroneous opinions, denies the opinions charged, or even his own written language. This is no bar to deliberation. *"Allegans contraria non est audiendus."* It rather concludes the case against him. A man may multiply denials and self-contradictions perpetually. This may be a reason why preamble and resolutions should not be adopted, upon a final vote, but it' is no reason why they should be declared as "out of order," nor is it any reason in support of the Presbytery's assumption of the Assembly's prerogative to decide constitutional law and bind it as a rule of action on the court. Again, I appeal to the acknowledged maxim of law, *" Ejus est interpretari, cujus est condere,"*—it belongs to that power to *interpret* the law, whose office it is to *settle and establish* it. To the General Assembly, therefore, composed of the representatives of Presbyteries, or in other words, to Presbyteries *in Assembly* by means of their representations, but not to Presbyteries individually, pertains this high prerogative. Otherwise, our Church would become a very Babel of multiplied and contradictory decisions upon questions of constitutional law, confusion worse confounded. The interpretation of the Assembly is binding law, and not the interpretation of the individual Presbytery.

The Presbytery's action assumed to interpret the clause in our Form of Government, Chapter X, Section 8, "to condemn erroneous opinions," etc., as meaning, that no court can condemn such opinions except by judicial arraignment of their author. But this exception is an interpolation of the constitution. It is an addition, an unauthorized gloss, not only in the face of a previous and discriminating clause as to *"judging ministers,"* a clause involving both the *person* and the *judicial process* together, but directly in face of contrary and binding decisions of our supreme court itself. Where does the constitution say, Moderator, that Presbyteries have no power to condemn erroneous opinions, except by the modal limitation of judicial process? Nowhere. That limitation defeats "the plain intent of the law," and is a mere *obiter dictum*, without the least authority. Not less unauthorized is the assertion that "the exercise of episcopal power is a usurpation of the judicial without submitting to its limitations." This is to deny both the letter of the constitution and the decisions of our supreme court. Judicial process is always the last resort and not the first. The Presbytery had no right to put *its* interpretation upon the constitution in face of the Assembly's interpretation of our law, already given.

And this was the doctrine of the very Assembly of 1834 itself. In the most express terms that Assembly affirmed, that to the General Assembly alone it belongs to *interpret* the constitution. It said these words, " the Form of Government vests the right of deciding questions of constitutional law, not in Synods, *but in the General Assembly.*" Moore's Digest, p. 263 (3). According to this announcement, no inferior court and no moderator may assume this prerogative and bind a new interpretation on the court as a rule of action. The thing to be specially remarked, just here, is this, that the very Assembly of 1834, which gave a wrong *interpretation* of the clause, " to condemn erroneous opinions which injure the peace and purity of the Church," by construing said clause with an unauthorized limitation, was the very Assembly which yet maintained that the *Supreme court alone* is competent to interpret the constitution and bind that interpretation as a rule of action on all our courts.

Precisely the same doctrine was reaffirmed by the Old School General Assembly of 1844, six years after the division. It said these words: " What interest has the Synod more than other Synods or Presbyteries in giving a wrong exposition of our book. When we *interpret* our constitution, the voice of the whole Church should be heard." (Moore's Digest, p. 598 (3). Thus, both the Old School and the New School brethren agreed in this, that the prerogative of interpreting our constitution and binding the interpretation upon all the courts, as a rule of action, *belongs to the General Assembly alone.* And all the more is this evident as we learn, from our supreme decisions, that no complaint will lie, in any case, against a court for declining to usurp this function of the Assembly (Moore's Digest, p. 598 (4), but that it will lie against the exercise of this function. (Moore's Digest, p. 593 (4). Thus, the general law maxim, " *Ejus est interpretari cujus est condere,*" the constitution itself, in its literal, rational and historical construction, brethren of both Old and New School alike, with the binding decisions of our Digest and its historical precedents, all show that the Cincinnati Presbytery, in the action I complain of, usurped the high prerogative of the General Assembly.

(4.) The fourth reason in support of my first point of Complaint is (see first point of Complaint), " that the action of Presbytery was *the turning of a constitutional question into a parliamentary rule of order,* so inventing a new rule in derogation of my constitutional and parliamentary rights."

Moderator, what do we mean when we use the expressions "law" and "order?" Is each one pleonastic of the other? Or, is there a well-defined and settled distinction between them? True, in a general and wide sense, law is a rule of action. But when we use it in the expression, "law and order," what is it we mean by *law*, and what by *order*, each as distinguished from the other, in deliberative bodies? The conceptions are totally different. By "law" we mean, our constitution, an organic statute, or a decision of the supreme court. Our Confession of Faith, Form of Government, Book of Discipline, Catechisms, Directory of Worship, and the decisions of the General Assembly, are what we call "*law.*" By "order" we mean, conformity to a prescribed mode of procedure in business in a deliberative body, and nothing more. When we say *law*, the mind goes straight to the constitution and its authorized interpretation. When we say *order*, the mind goes straight to parliamentery rules of procedure in business. The termini of the two conceptions, and the contents of the two, are totally different. The one relates wholly to the constitution and its interpretation, the other relates wholly to the general rules of our judicatories for procedure in business—it relates to "*proceedings*"—and such is the definition of lexicographers and parliamentarians. Mr. Webster's definition of "order" is as follows: "Adherence to the point in discussion according to established rules of debate; as the member is not in order, *i. e.*, he wanders from the question." "Established mode of proceeding;—the motion is not in order." "Regularity; settled mode of operation." The definition in Jefferson's Manual is as follows: "Order in conformity with the *rules* of order laid down. Departure from the rules, is a breach of order." In that majestic volume of a thousand pages by Mr. Cushing, on the "Law and Practice of Legislative Assemblies," founded on Hatsell's celebrated precedents, we have the following clear and unambiguous words: "All questions of order are determined by reference to the *rules* of order. Any member, rightfully in possession of the house, his motion having been seconded, is *in order.*" "And it is the right of members to originate propositions, at their pleasure, for the consideration of the house; and any member, in possession of the house, may make any motion he thinks proper."

Now, Moderator, where in all our rules of order is the interpretation of the constitution according to the Assembly of 1834 to be found? Where is our constitution found in the rules of order? Where are any of the decisions of any of our General Assemblies found in the rules of order? And by what right did the Presbytery of Cincinnati make *its* interpretation of the constitution a rule of order, and, upon that ground, rule my Preamble and Resolutions as "*out of order?*" The thing is too evident to require discussion. *Nothing is a "point of order" in parliamentary debate which does not relate to accepted rules of order prescribed for procedure in business.* I was perfectly in order, according to the rules of our court, as I have already shown. I violated no parliamentary regulation, either at Glendale or at Cincinnati. My paper was before the house, written and seconded, no other business being before the body, and was just as much in order as the papers of Dr. Morris or those of Messrs. Ritchie, Hills, and Stanton. A man is in order, if he conforms to the parliamentary rules of procedure in business. He may be perfectly in order, while his motion may be perfectly unconstitutional, and his motion may be perfectly constitutional, while he himself is as perfectly "out of order." Therefore it was a usurpation of my rights, when a question of constitutional law was turned into a "point of order," entertained by the Moderator, and sustained by the Presbytery, so taking from me, both my constitutional and parliamentary rights to discuss my Preamble and Resolutions on their merits, and to adduce in their support the "facts" which had been introduced into the house by the official report of its own committee.

But it has been said, there are such things as "constitutional rules," and we have a right, therefore, to turn questions of constitutional law into "rules of order." The logic of this reasoning is as fallacious as the intuition of the facts is obscure. No calculus, known to mathematics to-day, is able to fix the amount of power necessary to draw such an enormous conclusion, and no logical harness, yet made, is strong enough to endure the strain. For, "constitutional rules" relate to polity, and are parts of the constitution itself. They are actual amendments to, or interpretations of, the Articles of Government and Discipline, in every case, however, "excluding alteration of the doctrine and fundamental principles of the Church." (Moore's Digest, p. 328.) Proposed to all the Presbyteries and adopted, upon overture, by two thirds of them, they are then, formally, declared by the Assembly to be *law*, and are irrepealable, henceforth, by the Assembly itself or by any subordinate court. They are legislative acts of the whole Church. Presbytery can not make them, nor unmake them; neither can Assembly. As part of the constitution, they have the whole force of constitutional law. These rules are of the nature of judicial order of proceeding definitely defined, which, though not parliamentary rules of order, are defined order itself. Clearly, a motion against any of these could not be entertained, for here law and order are made identical. Where the constitution itself, as in judicial process, assumes the feature of a mandate, an express "shall," it is then settled order itself, and no motion can be entertained against it, making it out of order. The *ground* of refusal to entertain such motion, is not that the motion is unconstitutional, however true that may be, but that it is against order itself, and no motion is in order that is out of order.

Nor are our Rules of Order part of our Constitution. In express terms our Digest says: "The following rules, not having been submitted to the Presbyteries, *make no part of the Constitution of the Presbyterian Church.*" (Moore's Digest, p. 204.) And even if they did, yet, such a rule as the one the Cincinnati Presbytery has legislated into existence, on the basis of 1834, has no place in the catalogue. But now, we have been suddenly presented with a new rule of procedure, we may call it Rule XLIV, added to the list, and it will read this way : "*No Presbytery shall consider any motion, preamble or resolution, condemning erroneous opinions under its jurisdiction which injure the peace and purity of the Church, unless after judicial process of the author of said opinions.*" The odor of it, Moderator, savors very much of an attack upon the constitution indeed, but then, you know, it is only a "*rule of order!*" I admit, Moderator, that under such an enactment, my Preamble and Resolutions would have been out of order, but I deny that the Assembly has made such an enactment, or bound such a rule upon the court. Where is such a rule to be found, even in our constitutional rules ? Where is the Presbytery's right to turn a question of constitutional law, in face of the binding decision of the Assembly, into a rule of order? It is pure legislation, an assumption, by Presbytery, of the function of the General Assembly ; a violation of the dearest and most sacred rights of motion and discussion, guaranteed to every Presbytery by the constitution of the Presbyterian Church, and by parliamentary rule. How often must it be repeated before we understand it, that nothing is a "point of order" which does not relate to established rules of order prescribed for procedure in business.

But now, Moderator, granting that all I have said goes for nothing; admit, for the sake of argument, the unconstitutionality of my Preamble and Resolutions ; allow that the Presbytery's construction of the constitution was right, as against the binding decisions of the General Assembly ; grant that there is no such thing as non-judicial power to condemn error ; grant everything that the brethren opposed to my motion maintained, or might maintain, I still deny that a man is "*out of order*" simply because his motion or preamble and resolutions either are, or assumed to be, "*unconstitutional.*" You may lay them on the table, or vote them down, after they have been moved, seconded and discussed, even though they declare that the constitution itself is unconstitutional. But the mover is "in order," and has both a constitutional and a parliamentary right to be heard on their merits.

In support of this position I adduce the testimony of several gentlemen of eminent authority in parliamentary experience. The first I mention is the Hon. J. F. Follett, late Speaker of the House of Representatives of the State of Ohio.

CINCINNATI, O., October 9, 1876.
HON. J. F. FOLLETT:

DEAR SIR—The *constitution* of the Presbyterian Church, Form of Government, Chapter X, Section 8, gives a Presbytery the *"power to condemn erroneous* opinions that injure the peace and purity of the Church. Suppose I offer the following :

" WHEREAS, A. B. has taught and teaches so and so, which is "erroneous" (here I quote the proofs of error in language of the author), therefore,

" *Resolved,* That A. B. is in error in said opinions, and is hereby enjoined not to propagate them.

I. Is this preamble and resolution " OUT OF ORDER" if it is duly moved, seconded, and the mover has the floor, and there is no other business before the house?

II. Suppose some one rises to what he chooses to call a *"point of order,"* viz.: That according to *his interpretation* of the constitution, the above clause excludes the condemnation of error, except in the abstract, and that forty General Assemblies have so decided, and therefore it is *"out of order"* even to "consider" the preamble and resolution, is the the mover *"out of order"* on that account?

Is any interpretation of the constitution, *pro* or *con,* to be made a parliamentary rule for procedure in business? Admit that the Preamble and Resolution are against the constitution itself, most clearly, does that make their mover *" out of order,"* and close his mouth on the merits of the case?

Suppose a member of the legislature moves to burn up the constitution of the State, or to secede from the Union, and the motion is seconded, and the mover has a right to the floor, is he *"out of order"* because he is unconstitutional? Is he not entitled to speak to the full merits of the case, even though the house will vote down his resolutions instantly?

I hold that the "constitution" is one thing and "order" is another. Order in a deliberative body, is conformity to a prescribed mode of procedure in business and relates wholly to parliamentary rule, while

constitution or organic law is a wholly different thing, and no interpretation of it may be made a parliamentary rule under which to
declare a resolution opposed to that interpretation as "*out of order*,"
if it is duly seconded and the member has a right to the floor and no
other business is before the house? Please inform me, is my view
right or wrong?

Truly yours, etc., etc.,

*   *   *   *

"*I have no hesitation in saying your view is right.*

John F. Follett."

1. Does the unconstitutionality of a motion or preamble and resolution make said motion or preamble and resolution, ipso facto, "*out
of order?*"

"*It does not.*

J. F. Follett."

2. Is an unconstitutional motion, preamble or resolution, if duly
seconded, no other business being before the house, "*in order*," and
debateable on its merits?

"*It is.*   Very truly,   /

J. F. Follett."

I also add the following answer from my respected friend, Hon.
Rufus King, President of the late convention of the State of Ohio,
assembled for the revision of its Constitution;—an answer written to the
same communication addressed to the Hon. Mr. Follett:

"Cincinnati, O., October 8, 1876.

"My Dear Sir—Unless precluded by some special rule of order, the
Presbytery was bound to entertain such a motion as yours. I do not
see how it can even be questioned. Nothing which has relation to the
laws, powers, or duties of the body, can be out of order, if not expressly
forbidden by the rules of order.

Yours very truly,

Rufus King."

I add also the following correspondence had with the Hon. Schuyler
Colfax, formerly Speaker of the House of Representatives, and President of the Senate, of the United States:

Cincinnati, O., November 1, 1876.

Hon. Schuyler Colfax:
Dear Sir—Allow me to ask your decision, as a parliamentarian,
upon the following questions: 1. Is it the province of a presiding
officer, or of any deliberative body, acting under written parliamentary

"Rules of Order," to make this or that assumed or real interpretation of the Constitution a "point of order," or a "rule of order," when said interpretation is no part of the "Rules of Order?" 2. Does the unconstitutionality of a proposition make it, *ipso facto*, "out of order?" 3. Is any motion, Preamble, or Resolution, even if unconstitutional, debateable on its merits, if duly offered and seconded, and not excluded by the specified class of "undebateable motions" known as such to parliamentarians? Please be so kind as to give me your opinion.

Very truly yours, etc., etc.,

* * * *

"SOUTH BEND, IND , November 7, 1876.

"DEAR SIR—Your letter has just reached me. In Congress, the presiding officers do *not* rule out questions on any grounds of unconstitutionality. This practice is supposed to be the true *inference* from the British rule laid down in Jefferson's Manual, Sec. 35. "If an amendment be proposed inconsistent with one already agreed to, it is fit ground for its *rejection* by the House; but it is not within the competence of the speaker to suppress it, as if it were against order; for were he permitted to draw questions of consistence within the *vortex of order*, he might usurp a negative on important modifications and suppress instead of subserve the legislative will."

Respectfully yours,
SCHUYLER COLFAX."

I also add the following correspondence with the Hon. Edward McPherson, for many years Clerk of the National House of Representatives and a universal authority on parliamentary law and precedent throughout the country.

CINCINNATI, O., October 9, 1876.

HON. EDWARD MCPHERSON:

DEAR SIR—Our Form of Government, Chap. X, Sec. 8, with which you are well acquainted, gives Presbytery the "power," among other things, "to condemn erroneous opinions which injure the purity or peace of the Church." This is a function of Episcopal power, as I take it, discriminated from the function of Judicial power, which is involved in the previous clause, viz., of "judging ministers." My question is this, would a Preamble or, in other words, a proposition, introduced into Presbytery, reciting erroneous doctrines or views propagated by any of its ministers, with the necessary proofs therefor, taken from official documents on the table, or otherwise, and an appended Resolution condemning the error and enjoining its new propagation, be "out of order" or "unconstitutional?" And would an amendment, unconstitutional in itself, be "out of order" on that ground? To what extent does the jurisdiction of a parliamentary officer go? May any proposition or motion duly made and seconded be debated on its merits, if within the rules as to debateable motions? A brief answer to these interrogations will place me under obligations to your kindness.

Very sincerely yours, etc.,

* * *

"GETTYSBURG, PA., Nov. 10, 1876.

"DEAR SIR—I have been from home for several weeks and your letter of the 9th October did not reach me till after the 19th.

"Please excuse the delay of this reply. I believe I understand your point.

"As to the amendment. An amendment to a pending proposition, germane to it, is in order, without any regard to the alleged unconstitutionality. A presiding officer never undertakes to pass upon the *effect* of an amendment. His jurisdiction is wholly confined to the parliamentery questions of germaneness, degree, etc.

"As to the proposition. Any proposition duly offered and properly pending is subject to debate upon its merits, within the rules, as well if it be clearly unconstitutional, or if only presumably so. To deny this would be seriously to fetter all deliberative proceedings.

With great respect,
Truly yours,
EDWARD McPHERSON."*

Fortified by such testimony as the above, I maintain, therefore, (1.) That by "*order*" is meant conformity to prescribed "*rules of order*" for procedure in business; (2.) That nothing is a "*point of order*" which does not relate to these rules; (3.) That our parliamentary rules of order are no part of our constitution; (4.) That constitutional rules are no part of the rules of order; (5.) That Presbytery had no right to *interpret* the constitution, bind its interpretation upon the court, and turn it into a rule of order; (6.) That Presbytery had no right to legislate a new rule into existence conflicting with the binding decision of the Assembly; (7.) That a man is always "*in* order" when he conforms to the rules of order, and only "*out* of order" when he departs from the same; (8.) That a man may be perfectly "in order" when his motion is utterly *un*constitutional, and his motion may be perfectly *con*stitutional, when the man himself is utterly "out of order."

I need say no more on this first point of complaint. I complain that the dearest right of a Presbyterian minister, protected by a true construction of the constitution and by parliamentary rules, to both which I conformed, were taken from me, on the floor of the Presbytery, by an arbitrary decision of that body, and this action I submit to the judgment of the Synod.

II. The second point of Complaint is against the Presbytery's action, in accepting, and thereby making official documents of, the Special Report and collaterals of the Committee of Investigation in the case of

---

* The communications from Mr. Colfax and Mr. McPherson I did not receive till after the meeting of Synod. I have taken the liberty to insert them in the speech.   - T. II. S.

Mr. McCune, " *without any action whatever to amend or to rectify statements, judgments, and personalities therein contained, at variance with Righteousness and Truth.*" This, of course, relates *wholly to myself* and *the Presbytery.* I complain of no statements, judgments, or personalities, in reference to any one else.

(1.) The first reason in support of this second point of Complaint is, "That the Report opens with, and its recommendations rest upon, statements *contrary to truth.*"

(a.) It says, my Resolution, offered at Glendale, and printed in my pamphlet, was a "Resolution *censuring Mr. McCune.*" This is not true. The Resolution simply asked Presbytery to "reject the principles" Mr. McCune has advocated, and to say that the "*course pursued*" is in "*contravention*" of our law, and "*inconsistent*" with membership in our body. It relates wholly to *things,* proper to be acted upon by the episcopal power of the body. It proposes no "*censure*" of the *person,* not even an admonition. It implies no censure whatever. It is just what our Church has done scores of times, without censure, and repeats every time upon "review and control" of Records, and in public deliverances whenever necessary.

(b.) It says my pamphlet made "light' of the Committee and its work." In no paragraph, sentence, or clause of my pamphlet, can a syllable be found authenticating such a charge, or reflecting in the slightest degree upon the "*the Committee and its work.*" The statement is wholly gratuitous.

(c.) It says, that my pamphlet "*contains the staple and authority for the rumors existing against Mr. McCune.*" This also is untrue. My pamphlet was itself the product of "rumors," and of various publications, as also of previous discussions, long before the pamphlet was born ; and this was well known to the Committee. It was neither the staple, nor the authority, "*for* the rumors existing," at the time of its publication, nor at the time of Presbytery's appointment of its Committee. And none knew this better than the draftsman of the Report, Dr. J. G. Montfort. The pamphlet was published about two weeks after the Presbytery arose at Glendale, April 13, 1876. Now then, Moderator, I affirm that Mr. McCune's book on "Organic Union " was published in 1866, and has since been fully circulated. The "Christian Unity," edited by Mr. McCune, appeared in November, 1873. Dr. Monfort's adverse criticism upon the principles of that paper appeared in the same month, saying : "It will be seen that Bro. McCune aims at a great change in the Churches." In August, 1875, this same widely-circulated paper contained an editorial by the drawer of the report. He says, in that editorial, among other things : " If these brethren are for organization and association, or are already organized and associated, the external bond of union being the convention or association which met in New York in 1873, in Cincinnati in 1874, and in Suffolk, Va., in 1875, *we are at a loss to understand* how Mr. McCune or Mr. Mellish can be willing to maintain connection with the Presbyterian or Baptist Church. We should suppose that each would pass at once for an old organization that is unauthorized and extra-scriptural to a new one on a New Testament Basis." "The Address to all Christian Ministers and Churches in North America" was issued in 1874. A long debate between Mr. McCune and the Christian Standard occurred in 1875 and the earlier part of 1876. The L. and M. L. "Declaration and Basis," and the Council were in the latter part of 1875; and the Herald and Presbyter published the proceedings, as did other papers. Public discussions by Messrs. McCune, Morris, Skinner, and Layman, besides, occurred in the Cincinnati Gazette, Commercial, and Times, also discussions in the Christian Observer, the United Presbyterian, Interior, the Presbyterian, the Journal and Messenger, the North-western Christian Advocate, and other papers, all which I present as evidence for the point I make, before ever the Glendale Presbytery met, or my pamphlet saw the light. An interlocutory meeting had even been proposed in reference to this matter. The opening sentences of my pamphlet are themselves a refutation of the Committee's statement. The resolution of the Presbytery under which the Committee was appointed, and beginning thus, "Wheras, for *some time past* there have been current rumors," etc., —a form of expression penned by the drawer of the report himself,—seals the allegation of the Committee as untrue. With what conscience, then, or with what sense of justice or of truth, could the drawer of the report and the Committee base their report upon the false statement that my pamphlet was the "*staple and authority for the rumors existing,*" in "*time past,*" and into which they were appointed to inquire, before the pamphlet was born? On this I need say no more, except that nothing could be more unjust or untrue than the attempt to make me the author of Common Fame; a device contrived (1), to cut away any Presbyterial action on the ground of Common Fame in the case, and (2) to lay the ground that I be required to become a responsible prosecutor. Thus does the report of the Committee open with, and its recommendations rest upon, three unfounded statements.

(2.) The second reason in support of the second point of Complaint is, that this accepted report steps out of its way to *raise a new case,* instead of confining itself to the terms of the resolution under which the Committee was appointed." This policy, in the light of the preceding untruthfulness, was evidently to my damage before the public and was beyond the province of the Committee. The terms of that resolution were, to have a "full conference with Mr. McCune," and to inquire into all the "*facts*" bearing on the "*case*" of Mr. McCune, and report to Presbytery. Under these instructions the Committee assumes to pronounce upon me personally and upon the publication of my pamphlets, written in defense of my rights as a Presbyter, and of the faith and order of the Church, a condemnatory judgment. It recommends that I be dealt with for publishing the pamphlet. My mouth having been closed in the Glendale Presbytery, I am to be dealt with for opening it outside of the Presbytery, and then have it closed again on the merits of the case when the Presbytery met thereafter. It recommends that Presbytery take action to the effect that I either "prove or retract" certain picked statements by Mr. McCune, and that I "*ought*" so to do, in default of which, it suggests a prosecution for "*slander.*" Was this, Moderator, the work the Committee was sent to do under the terms of the resolution, recommending no action whatever in the case it was appointed to examine, and the material "facts" of which case it was required to present to the Presbytery. It turned aside to do as I have intimated. I submit that this was an unlawful exercise of the functions of the Committee, in the interest of a personal attack upon myself. And yet Presbytery accepted all this without a word of rebuke or official correction.

(3.) The third reason in support of the second point of Complaint is, "That it implies a censure on the undersigned and recommends the Presbytery to pass a judgment which also implies a censure." Censure for publication, censure in case I declined to "prove or retract." It says I "*ought*" to do one or the other, that is, I am under moral obligation to do this, and in case I do not, then a prosecution for "slander" may be the next appropriate step! What is all this, Moderator, but an implied "censure" of me personally? All this, I affirm, was beyond the province of the Committee under the terms of its instructions; and against this unprecedented liberty I complain, as also against the formal acceptance of such a report, giving it the sanction of an official document. I hold as firmly as any man can, that a public slanderer "ought" to prove or retract, and that no apologies short of this "ought" to be accepted. Ministerial character is too precious to be trifled with.

(4.) The fourth reason in support of the second point of Complaint is, "That part of the Collaterals of the Report indulge in *gross personalities* against the undersigned, which would not be tolerated for one moment in debate, and ought not to be tolerated in an official document."

The Collaterals are specified by the Committee in their Special Report, and are expressly said by them to be a "part of our report." What they contain was well known to Dr. Monfort, the Chairman of the Committee, and to the Committee itself. I think it will be difficult for any one to show wherein I personally have violated the first principles of Christian courtesy or gentlemanly respect, by the use of opprobious and vituperative epithets against any one. I have sought simply to defend the faith and order of my Church, in a manly and Christian way. But the Report of the Committee has introduced into the Presbytery an array of gross personalities, the parallel to which can not be found in any official document, secular or political, in the country. Collateral No. 1, p. 5, "violent, unlawful and slanderous assault;" "attacked and villified," p. 6; "unrighteous attempt," p. 6; "proposed to reach this high-handed and tyrannical result," p. 7; "assailing me with a great mass of quotations of garbled phrases," p 7; "shameful unfairness," p 7; "flagrantly unjust," "slanderous," "defiant," "disrespectful to the lawful jurisdiction of the Presbytery," "frantic outcry," p. 8; "slanderous charges," "crying injustice," p. 10; "unprecedented in the history of slander," p. 5. Collateral No. 4, "violent, unlawful and contumacious assault," p. 1; "recklessly and officiously asserts," p. 5; "defamatory pamphlet," "tyrannical and false assumption," p. 5 Collateral No. 5, "untrue and slanderous statements," p. 3; "defamer," "shamefully untrue statements," p. 4; "shameful and outrageous wrong," p. 12; "violently contumacious and defamatory statements," p. 26.

Moderator, I blush for my Church. I blush for the degeneracy of manners that prevails in our midst, and for that demoralization of Christian sentiment and propriety which could allow our ears to be shocked by such things in a court of the Lord Jesus Christ. I hang my head in shame. I complain righteously to this body. Personalities, sir, are the order of the day, and it is time that the Church of Christ set its face like a flint against the enormity. It pleased my ear, I must say it in justice to some of my brethren, to hear their expressions of indignation at the character of the Report, styling it "outrageous," "horrid," and "unparalleled in the history of the Church." But that the Presbytery itself, under the lead of those who controlled it, should tolerate and accept such a Report without rebuke, tells its own story.

III. The third point of Complaint is against the action of Presbytery, in "adopting an answer to the protest of the undersigned, Sep.

tember 15th, 1876, Mt. Auburn, *without rectifying its erroneous state-ments and the false impression it is calculated to make.*"

(1.) My first reason in support of this third point of Complaint is, "*That* said answer does *not accurately represent the facts of the case.*" My second reason in support of the third point is, that "*it represents the undersigned as being out of order* and furnishing reasonable grounds for the annoyances and unlawful interruptions under which he was forced to retire from the floor of the Presbytery." My third reason is, "that *no withdrawal* of the protest for alteration, on account of mis-representation in the answer, could make the protest "more agree-able" to the "views" of the undersigned." I take these three reasons together, and for the first two of them adduce the public reports of the occurrences at Mt. Auburn, certified to, as correct reports, by the gentlemen of the press who made them. I also present my Protest and the Answer of the Presbytery to the same. (Here read the Gazette and Commercial reports.)

Now, Moderator, I make the following points: (1.) I was ruled as in order, by the Chair, when reading the Special Report of the Inves-tigating Committee. (2.) I never traversed that report with "unlim-ited" range, as the protest insinuates. I confined myself, in the first place, strictly to the *Special* Report; and in the second place, closely to one paragraph of that report, printed as No. 2 in the Ga-zette, reading it from the print. I had read precisely *one inch and three quarters* by actual measurement, during over an hour's patient and protracted effort to go on under the ruling of the Moderator. I sought to read nothing else, and I will read now just what I read then. (Here read.) This is all, sir. There is nothing else in that report that touched the question in hand. It is therefore untrue that I was indulging in "unlimited reading," or that the Moderator called me to order on that account. (3.) All Mr. McCune's objections and in-terruptions were directly to the point, that I had *no* right to read that part of the report which the Moderator ruled I *had* a right to read, in order to show that the Committee was as much bound to prosecute Mr. McCune as I was. (4.) I was never called to order once by the Moderator, or as ruled out of order. The Moderator's remarks, that I would confine myself to the question and the paper, were remarks made in the midst of boundless confusion, *not as calls of myself to order*, but as simple repetitions and assurances to the court that, in what I should say and read, I must confine myself to the paper and to the ques-tion, both which I did, not that I had transgressed in a single instance. (5.) The inch and three quarters that I did read was germane to the matters involved in the motion under discussion, as the whole paragraph was, and this I was proceeding to show, but was prevented by persistent interruptions, which were not restrained. They coincided with "the particular matters" complained of, but I was not allowed to go on and show this fact. (6.) The drawer of the Report affirmed to me personally, in my study, after the Presbytery was over, that I had a perfect right to read that whole paragraph, which is six inches long in print, and that I ought to have been allowed a still larger range. It is not true, therefore, as I have shown, that I sought an "unlimited" range, or that I was out of order, or that I wandered from the question, or that I did anything not pertinent to the discussion, or that I trespassed the ruling of the Chair, or that my conduct gave any just ground for the unlawful interruptions to which I was subjected, or that in nearly or quite every instance, the Moderator found it necessary to warn me to keep within his ruling, all which the answer to the protest alleges as true, and the contrary of which I allege. The simple fact is this, the determination on the part of several individuals was, that that part of the Committee's report which I was reading should not be read and I was forced to retire, under protest that I was not protected in my rights. And now, in face of such allegations as the above, in the answer to the protest, it must be evident to every one, that *no withdrawal* of my protest by myself, could make it "more agreeable" to my "views" or to the facts in the case, or to my vindication against the false impeachments of the answer, by any alteration that I might make, and therefore my only resort is, to complain to this body against the injustice that has been done.

And thus do I sum up the whole case of which I complain : A case of grievous injustice against a man who has simply sought to draw the notice of his Presbytery, in these days of demoralization in this region, to endangering error and practice, under the disguise of a false unionism and liberalism, which repels the distinctive tenets of our creed, and the enforcement of denominational law. Injustice in violation of my constitutional and parliamentary rights, both which have been twice wrested from me on the floor of the Presbytery, bound to protect me in the same ; injustice in accepting the Committee's Report, which opens with, and rests upon, three separate statements of untruth ; injustice in seeking to make me the author of the "rumors" which, "in time past," had spread over the country, before even my pamphlet was born ; injustice in turning aside to institute a new case, and pronounce on the basis of those untruths a censuring judgment against me personally, as also against the public defense of my rights as a Presbyter, and of the faith and order of the Presbyterian Church ; injustice in asserting that I was under moral obligation either to

" prove or retract ; " injustice in recommending a judicial investigation of certain selected statements, on Mr. McCune's representation alone, as if my quotations or argument were false on that account; injustice for suggesting a prosecution for " slander" in case I declined to accede to the imputation in the judgment, that I ought to " prove or retract;" injustice in accepting collaterals to the report, and making them official documents, when they abounded in gross personalities and multiplied vituperative epithets, not tolerated even in the councils of unconverted men; injustice in representing me as a persistent breaker of the order of my Presbytery, a constant trespasser upon the ruling of the Chair, and the author of the very disorder and confusion under which I was forced to retire from the floor of the Presbytery; a twelve-fold injustice, repeated, protracted, accumulated, and which I here bring and lay before the bar of this Synod, and upon which I ask the judgment of my brethren, and all this injustice, oppression and wrong, in an effort to avoid and delay the bounden duty of the Presbytery, to attend to the disorders which, by common fame, had been circulated through the country.

But, Moderator, high over all personal injustice and wrong, looms the great question of the Episcopal or Paternal Power of the Presbytery to condemn error in doctrine and practice, apart from judicial process, and so conserve the faith and order of the Church. This power, expressly vested in the Presbytery, and in all our courts, by Christ, the Head of the Church, and engraved in the constitution itself, Cincinnati Presbytery has repudiated. It is a dangerous relapse. To the Presbyterian Church, to-day, as ever, belongs the whole power of the apostolic Church, save its miraculous and extraordinary to oversee and govern the flock of God, a plenary power administered in fidelity centuries before our forms of " actual process " were recorded. To each minister of the Presbyterian Church belongs the whole ordinary power of the apostles, to watch, govern and direct, to reprove, rebuke and exhort with all, long suffering and doctrine, apart from judicial forms. Who will say that the Presbytery has not the inherent power which belongs inherently to each minister and elder who composes it? Sir, it is more than a fallacy to say that the doctrine and order of the house of God can not be protected under our constitution, except by forensic process. The prophets contradict it. The New Testament contradicts it. The apostolic example contradicts it. The practice of the Church in every age contradicts it. Every apostolic epistle is a loud protest against it. The history of the Presbyterian, and every other Evangelical Church in Christendom, contradicts it. And woe to the Church of Christ, the day when she puts herself at the mercy of every tenacious inventor of doctrine, or every reviver of heresies exploded a thousand times, who makes use of her standards to shackle her freedom, and dares her to move one step in vindication of her creed, unless at the expense of perpetual judicial war. Sir, my heart and my head alike are in this great matter; I want to save the anchor. I would have my brethren pause, in this our great Church, whose limits extend so wide, and remember that maxim consecrated by so much illustration: "TIMES OF UNION ARE TIMES OF PERIL FOR THE TRUTH." And I would have them consider, too, the significance of that other maxim, printed so clearly and legibly on the page of church history, viz.: "That every schismatic demands a trial!" But, Moderator, if the genius of our constitution is eminent in anything, it is in this, that the mission of the Church is to bear testimony to the truth of Christ, and that it is the bounden duty of the Presbytery, apart from forensic forms, to condemn errors in doctrine and practice, under its own jurisdiction, which injure the unity, peace and purity of the Church. The failure to do this was the source of either increasing corruption on the one hand, by reason of neglect, or of perpetual war on the other, by reason of effort herein. First and last, it is the "heavenly doctrine" and "heavenly order" we prize above all. Condemn the error in doctrine and the irregularity in practice by the episcopal power vested by Christ in the ministry of His Church. Rebuke and exhort, *admonish* and warn. *Enjoin* all not to propagate what is fatal to truth and order. If contumacy follows, the remedy is at hand, without years of contention, agony, resistance, and regret.

Moderator and brethren, I thank you; I feel I have discharged a sacred duty to God, to my Church, to Christ, to you, in bringing this matter before you. My conscience is at rest. My heart beats warm in hope that God will bring good out of this contest. Were it in my hand to do it, I would arrest every unnecessary judicial process for false doctrine, everywhere, and I would call upon every court of the Lord Jesus to stand to its responsibility in the exercise of legitimate episcopal power, condemning erroneous opinions and practices, so preserving to the Church her noble polity and creed, and, at the same time, her unity, purity and peace.

PROTEST.

" *To the Synod of Cincinnati:*

" DEAR BRETHREN—The undersigned hereby protests against the action of the Synod of Cincinnati, taken at its annual session, October 23, 1876, in adopting the following preamble and resolutions, to wit:

" WHEREAS, The issuing of the complaint of Dr. Skinner, as recommended by the Judicial Committee, *may* prejudice the case now known as the McCune case, at present pending before the Cincinnati Presbytery; therefore,

" *Resolved,* That the *consideration of the report of the Judicial Committee* upon the said complaint of Dr. Skinner, be and is hereby *postponed* until the issue of the case of Mr. McCune by said Presbytery."

My reasons for this protest, are:

"1. Because my rights to a present hearing upon the merits of my particular case, which I have closely and carefully discriminated from any possible relation to the possible case of Mr. McCune, not yet framed, and belonging to another court, is guaranteed to me by the provisions of the constitution, all the conditions necessary as to this having been by me fulfilled.

"2. Because the argument of the Preamble, that the present hearing of my complaint in this court, utterly distinct from a case not yet framed, nor presented to another and lower court, would be just as good in the lower court against the hearing of Mr. McCune's case, when it shall be presented, if any such connexion exists between them as the Preamble assumes. Each case must stand upon its own merits, and each court must judge for itself.

"3. Because the Synod had no official knowledge of my complaint, while its character was misrepresented by individuals, the complaint itself never having been so much as read, and equally, has no official knowledge of the case, yet to be, of Mr. McCune. The Judicial Committee, in neither of its reports, either described my complaint, or made a solitary quotation from it.

"4. Because the Judicial Committee had unanimously reported that my complaint was 'in order,' and had been regularly conducted, and recommended that it be taken up by the Synod, and the Synod voted to take up my complaint.

"5. Because even a refusal to consider the Judicial Committee's 'report,' as the resolution has it, and which declared that my complaint was 'in order,' is not only a refusal by the Synod to hear now my complaint, and to which hearing I have a perfect right, but is a refusal to decide, even now, *whether there is any complaint at all by me regularly in order before this body, and entitled now to be heard.* It was a practical ejection of my complaint from the Synod.

" 6. Because it is a repetition, now the third time during six months, of the very thing of which I complain to this body as previously twice practiced upon me in the court below, viz: The setting aside of my present constitutional rights by the exercise of an assumed discretionary power, excluded by the provisions of the constitution itself in all cases where such rights are involved.

" For these reasons I respectfully protest, and give notice of complaint to the General Assembly.

"Yours fraternally,

" THOMAS H. SKINNER."

" LEBANON, O., Oct. 24, 1876."

NOTICE OF COMPLAINT TO THE GENERAL ASSEMBLY.

" *To the Moderator of the Synod of Cincinnati :*

" The undersigned hereby respectfully gives notice of his complaint to the General Assembly, against the following action of the Synod of Cincinnati, October 23, 1876, to wit :

"' WHEREAS, The issuing of the complaint of Dr. Skinner, as recommended by the Judicial Committee, may prejudice the case, now known as the McCune case, at present pending before the Cincinnati Presbytery; therefore,

"' *Resolved*, That the consideration of the report of the Judicial Committee upon the said complaint of Dr. Skinner be, and hereby is, postponed until the issue of the case of Mr. McCune by said Presbytery.'

" My reasons for this complaint are :

" First, Because the above action excluded the undersigned from a hearing on his complaint to which he was entitled both by constitutional and parliamentary law.

" Second, Because the preamble specifying the ground of the Synod's action offered no good and sufficient showing for setting aside the vested ecclesiastical rights of the undersigned.

" Third, Because such action is an encouragement of insubordination in the lower courts, and is destructive, not only of individual rights, but of the peace, purity, and unity of the Church.

" OCTOBER 27, 1876.   " THOMAS H. SKINNER."

" The undersigned unite with the Rev. T. H. Skinner, D. D., in the above complaint to the General Assembly.

" T. CHARLES THOMAS,	NATHANIAL WEST,
" W. B. SPENCE,	R. H. LEONARD,
" HENRY W. BIGGS,	EDWARD H. CAMP,
" J. GAMBLE,	E. D. LEDYARD.
" L. H. LONG,	

ACTION OF THE SESSION OF THE SECOND PRESBYTERIAN CHURCH.

" ' *Resolved*, that the session of the Second Presbyterian Church of Cincinnati, in full sympathy with our Pastor in his efforts to maintain the faith and order of the Presbyterian standards, and to secure respect by the lower courts for vested ecclesiastical rights, unite with him in his complaint to the General Assembly."

" OCTOBER 30, 1876."

" J. BURNET JR., *Clerk of Session.*

" JAMES TAYLOR,	WM. H. NEFF,
" WM. H. ALLEN,	S. J. BROADWELL,
" E. H. PENDLETON,	WM. H. MUSSEY."

ACTION OF THE BOARD OF TRUSTEES.

" *Resolved,* That we, the undersigned, Trustees of the Second Presbyterian Church of Cincinnati, being in full accord and sympathy with our Pastor in his efforts to maintain the faith and order of the Presbyterian standards, and to secure respect by the lower courts for vested ecclesiastial rights, unite with him in his complaint to the General Assembly.

" NOVEMBER 6, 1876.

" WM. WOODS,	JOHN SHILLITO, *President.*
" GEO. WILSHIRE,	THORNTON M. HINKLE, *Sec.*
" JOHN A. MURPHY,	A. S. WINSLOW."
" G. P. GRIFFITH,	

ACTION OF THE DEACONS.

" *Resolved,* That the Deacons of the Second Presbyterian Church, of Cincinnati, in full sympathy with the Session, the Trustees and the Pastor, do cordially unite with the Pastor in the above complaint to the General Assembly.

" D. B. LUPTON,
" H. P. LLOYD,
" WM. HUBBELL FISHER,
" GEO. A. PRICHARD."

NOVEMBER 6, 1876.

" The undersigned, members and Elders of other Presbyterian Churches of the city of Cincinnati, also unite in the above complaint.

" F. T. LOCKWOOD,	W. W. SCARBOROUGH,
" FRANCIS FERRY,	H. STEWART,
" ALEX. M. JOHNSON,	GEO. W. MCALPIN,
" HUGH MCBIRNEY,	WM. CLENDENIN,
" RICHARD SMITH,	M. W. OLIVER,
" THEO. KEMPER,	IRA. HAYNES,
" JOHN W. CALDWELL,	J. C. BRADFORD.

www.ingramcontent.com/pod-product-compliance
Lightning Source LLC
Chambersburg PA
CBHW032117080426
42733CB00008B/975